Reading, Writing, and Leaving Home

The Curse of the Appropriate Man

House of Women

The Mirror

The Bungalow

Home Ground

Friends of the Family

READING, WRITING, AND LEAVING HOME

Life on the Page

LYNN FREED

HARCOURT, INC.

Orlando   Austin   New York   San Diego   Toronto   London

www.HarcourtBooks.com

The photos accompanying the stories "Doing Time" and
"Home on the Range" are by Mary Pitts and are reproduced with
her kind permission. The photo for "Taming the Gorgon" is by
Vicky Cass and is reproduced with her kind permission.

Library of Congress Cataloging-in-Publication Data
Freed, Lynn.
Reading, writing, and leaving home: a life on the page/
Lynn Freed.—1st ed.
p.   cm.
1. Freed, Lynn. 2. Authors, South African—20th century—Biography.
3. Authors, American—20th century—Biography. 4. English teachers—
United States—Biography. 5. South African Americans—Biography.
6. Fiction—Authorship. I. Title.
PR9369.3.F68Z47 2005
823'.914—dc22   2005002397
ISBN-13: 978-0-15-101132-2
ISBN-10: 0-15-101132-X

Text set in Garamond MT
Designed by Cathy Riggs

Printed in the United States of America

First edition
A C E G I K J H F D B

For Rosemary

Contents

Reading, Writing, and Leaving Home

A CHILD'S READING

O NLY LONG AFTER I WAS OLD ENOUGH to read for myself, did I really make the connection between literature and the printed word. My mother, whose first and abiding love was for the theatre, preferred to tell her own versions of the stories other parents read to their children from books. This way she could add characters at will, eliminate others, change the plot around, and thus string out the story into a series of episodic cliff-hangers that would last over a period of weeks or even months. The books themselves remained on our shelves, mouldy and full of bookworm in the hot, damp region of South Africa in which we lived.

The first story I remember her delivering was Charles Kingsley's *Water-Babies,* one of those strange English tales for children, in which bad people with money and foul tempers bully small, poor, helpless, good people, often children. Good does triumph in the end, of course, but not before lessons have been learned and the wicked punished. In this particular story, Tom is a very young chimney sweep, who is employed by the evil Mr. Grimes. Tom runs away, falls into a river, and meets there the water-babies of the title, with whom he takes up residence.

My mother, falling into an old literary trap, managed to make the evil characters, both above and below the water, far more appealing than Tom. As she came forth with yet another demon lying in wait for him, and he—too good to be true and a bit stupid—accomplished another narrow escape, I lay shivering with delight. When I finally came to read the book itself, with its angelic illustrations of the water-babies and even the rather predictably grumpy Mr. Grimes, I felt terribly let down. Not only was my mother's version better, but it seemed truer as well.

What I did take on faith in this story, however—and in so many other stories fed to South African children when I was growing up—was that, contrary to what was true in my world, small white boys could be made to work for a living (girls, too—to wit the many tales of English waifs dressed in rags, who skivvied all day and were then consigned to freezing London attics to pray and shiver through the night). Also that snow fell at Christmastime, that there were fires rather than flower arrangements in fireplaces, and that hedgehogs, toads, foxes, and moles—not monkeys, snakes, and iguanas, the urban animals of my childhood—were the sorts of creatures which, in fiction, would stand up on their hind legs, don clothing, and sally forth into a story.

More than this, I believed that these strange customs and creatures were more real than those of the world I lived in, and far more worthy of fiction. The real world of my childhood—a large subtropical port on the Indian Ocean, with beaches and bush and sugarcane and steaming heat, a strict Anglican girls' school, massive family gatherings on Friday nights and Jewish holidays, and then my parents' theatre world, the plays my mother directed, my father learning his lines every evening in the bath, both of them off to rehearsal night after night, leaving the next episode of her story for me to listen to on a huge reel-to-reel tape recorder—this world did not exist, not even peripherally, in the literature available to me. Nor did I think that it should.

What I did encounter of indigenous South African literature came later, much later, at school. There, the odd poem or book (Roy

Campbell, Laurens van der Post) would be included in an otherwise watertight English syllabus: Shakespeare, Jane Austen, Thackeray, Dickens, Hardy, and, of course, the King James Bible. There wasn't even any venturing into Bloomsbury or, across the Atlantic, to America, absolutely not. Our history teacher, who, like most of the teachers in the school was English, stopped short of teaching the First World War, which, said she in 1960, was still controversial.

The Africa of popular imagination came to us via the radio. Until the midseventies, there was no television in South Africa, and so it was radio that offered programs like *Tarzan of the Apes,* to which I listened every evening in the kitchen with the servants. There we stood in rapt silence next to the fridge, on top of which the wireless sat in a place of honour.

Meanwhile, the fact that I was learning to read did not bring my mother's nightly episodes to an end, far from it. She moved on to the Brothers Grimm, to Rudyard Kipling's *Just So Stories* (a world much more familiar to me than

Tarzan's jungle), to *The Wind in the Willows,* which never engaged me, not even her version of it, and then to the plays of J. M. Barrie — *Quality Street; Peter Pan;* and my favourite, *The Admirable Crichton.* These she told from the point of view of whichever character she herself happened to have played on the stage.

The books I was beginning to read for myself — by English children's author, Enid Blyton — were considered lower than comics by the local cognoscenti, chief among whom was one of my father's sisters, a psychologist. My mother, a natural foe to my father's family, to the whole idea of psychology, and, indeed, to censorship itself (except for Disney, which she would not countenance), lifted her ample nose in scorn. Blyton's books might trespass upon the rudimentary borders of correctitude being laid down, even then, by the likes of my aunt, but they had me reading for once, lying quietly on the verandah swing seat or down in the summerhouse, and then rushing back into the house to ask my mother to take a few more out of the library for me the next day.

What Blyton understood very well, even in her Noddy books for the very young, was the universal desire of children to escape from the sovereignty of adults. And so, the fact that Noddy had his own car, which, like him, was an animated toy, and that he made off in it with Big Ears, his friend, or that later, in Blyton's pre-adolescent novels, *Five Go Off in a Caravan, Hollow Tree House, The Naughtiest Girl in the School,* there were rebels and runaways and naughty children finding adventure beyond the pale — this freedom was a wonderful thing for a girl living at the bottom of Africa and dreaming of leaving herself one day, somehow, for the real world.

Unlike my mother, I was not a natural reader. I read slowly and quite haphazardly. As the youngest child in a large household of family and servants, I spent most of my time unsupervised, much of it outdoors. It was here that

I was most alive to adventure and fantasy, creating grandiose scenarios from the top of the mango tree or taking off on my bicycle to explore. With books it was different. I read when it was dark, when it rained, when I was sick, or when I felt like company.

Most of the books in the house were kept in my parents' study, a cosy room with leather chairs, teak bookshelves, leaded windows, and piles of scripts stacked around on the floor. It was there that my mother was to be found during the day, either timing scripts or drilling a new actor. And there that I was allowed to read whatever was available — mostly plays, but also opera libretti, the odd history, a few biographies, a selection of popular novels — as long as I didn't interrupt.

One day I came upon a collection of books I'd never noticed — right in the back corner, behind the piles of scripts. They were books on the Holocaust. As soon as I discovered their existence, I returned to them obsessively, reading book after book and then rereading them, looking up words I did not understand, scrutinising the horrifying photographs so that, even to this day, they are burned into memory.

In contrast to the comfortable remove at which I felt myself from the horrors of received children's fiction, nothing separated me from those of the Holocaust. They seemed quite able to reach off the shelf, out of a book, and swallow me. Other children I knew dreaded bogey-men under the bed, emblems, no doubt, of the revolution their parents expected to happen one day. My demons, however, were Nazis with guns and gas ovens. Having one's throat slit by the next-door neighbour's servant someday in the distant future seemed mild by comparison.

As I GREW older, my mother did not stop playing Mother Goose; she simply changed the old bedtime format. Driving along, she would tell me the story of a play she had just read, or a novel she was adapting for *Lux Radio Theatre,* or about an aunt, whose suitor had demanded a dowry that her mother had refused to pay and everyone had landed up marrying the wrong person and now look how unhappy they all were. I knew, of course, not to trust her version of things, but at the same time, over the years, I found myself reading a book or seeing a play or an opera in a kind of stereoscope: what was written, and then what could have happened, what should have happened.

Even when my mother was too old, blind, and confused either to read or to be read to, still she managed to see goblins with pointed hats lurking on the verandah, men riding up the drive-way on horseback, elegant ladies coming in for tea under the guise of her nurse. Together with so much else from her life—her husband, her home, and us, her audience—her text had van-ished. And so she was doing the best she could with what was left to her—the imagination.

HONORARY SON

I GREW UP WITH TWO OLDER SISTERS AND four shadow brothers. The shadows were the boys my mother did not have — five-month miscarriages, the last of which she suffered when I was five and she was forty-four or -five. There she lay in a lacy bed jacket, propped up in the hospital bed, her face composed into its familiar tragic look. And even then I knew I'd had a narrow escape.

The youngest girl in a family in which the only male is the father is fortunate. She combines the favoured status of youngest child with that of honorary son. And, although she is thought to be destined for some trouble with men in the future — tending towards failure in marriage and needing, it is suggested, an older, rich husband — still, she is relatively lucky in the absence of brothers.

In my case, the luck was complicated by the beauty of my sisters. The oldest looked like a Pre-Raphaelite angel—wide cheeks, green eyes, a full mouth, all crowned by a head of soft brown curls. The other was Mediterranean— olive skin, black eyes, black hair. Long before I was born, they were princesses in the family diorama. My mother dressed them in hand-smocked frocks and matching bloomers, little straw hats, crocheted socks, and shoes imported from England. When they weren't princesses, they were nymphs, running naked around the garden, in keeping with my parents' strongly held views on health and nudity. Or they were maenads, clawing at each other's flesh and eyes, screaming, crying—fighting, I would guess now, for top billing.

And then, after two of the shadow boys, I was born. Another female. And, as it turned out, rather plain. From the start, I was treated with amusement, like a sort of wild card. How did such a thing happen to us? But there I was— undemanding, as disappointments tend to be at first, and not unpleasant. And so I was left to romp along the edges in the hand-smocked hand-me-downs, happy, it seems, to have been included at all.

Most of what we think we remember of early childhood, we have made up or extrapolated from what others have told us. What I remember beyond what I have been told is a tremendous need to please, a talent for getting a laugh by playing the fool, and, most of all, an early passion for a special future of my own. How this latter would be accomplished, what, in fact, it would be, I had no idea. But there it was as I ran wild and naked around the garden, or built a tree house high in the mango tree, sat up there singing hymns and arias at the top of my voice. What I knew was that I wanted something magnificent for myself, something far away, in the real world, something quite different from what lay ahead for my sisters or for other girls I knew.

While I loved to watch my sisters sitting at their dressing tables, their skirts spread around them, inspecting their images in the mirror, I knew very early that what I wanted for myself had very little to do with the way I looked. Sturdy and strong, browned from the sun, I enjoyed a boy's sense of entitlement to his appearance. And to much else, too. I was restless and noisy. I interrupted. I showed off. I talked back. My sisters complained that I was spoiled, a pest. My parents laughed.

Quite soon after the last of the shadow boys, my father began to take me up as the honorary son of the family. Waylaid from a promising engineering career of his own and into a life of shopkeeping and amateur theatricals, he sug-

gested that I might consider a future in engineering myself. After all, I loved to build things,
didn't I? He brought out the Meccano set he'd
been given as a child and set it up for me on the
verandah table. He also lent me his tools, gave
me scraps of wood to work with. I had no interest in the Meccano set, but I did build a tree
house with his tools. I hammered hundreds of
nails into dozens of boards on any number of
pretexts.

My parents were enchanted. The bolder I
was, the better they liked it. And so I scaled the
palm trees that lined the fence, swinging out
from the tops. I climbed anything, in fact, even
the drainpipes, and danced on the loose tiles of
the roof. In a delirium of bravado, I once
jumped out of a very high upstairs window with
my eiderdown tied around my shoulders, land-
ing, unhurt, on the laundry lawn below.

I also became my mother's favourite. Clearly,
I resembled her. We shared the same long nose
in an oval face; the wide, dark eyes; and sudden,
furious temper. Very early, I had from her the

conviction that I was entitled to want be any-thing I wished, as long as my future included a husband ("someone with a brain to match yours"). There was also a bias towards the arts and away from professions like medicine ("a dull lot") or teaching ("what a waste of talent"). Whatever it was that I was to become, it should be something that could be printed triumphantly in the local newspapers. It should lead to calls of congratulations, interviews with the press, the whole family given ballast by me, the one who was more than just a woman.

My sisters, in the meantime, were blossoming teenage beauties, the oldest already well into a re-lationship with her future husband. With them, my mother concentrated on presentation. Like the most practised of madams, she instructed the alteration hand to lower that neckline, pinch in the waist. They squeezed themselves into merry widows and girdles, shaved their legs, curled their hair, concocted masks and bleaches out of egg whites and vinegar and soap flakes. I sat watch-ing from the bedroom chair as my mother pinned up a hem. I sat at her feet as she beaded a bodice with tiny seed pearls. "He won't be able to take his eyes off you," she would say to one or the other of them. "You'll see how people's heads will turn."

When my turn came eventually, there were no such assurances. My mother, wondering suddenly at what she had wrought, sent me off to ballet classes "to gain grace." My father, who was expert at stage makeup, instructed me on how to disguise the length of my nose, how to suggest the cheekbones under my broad, fleshy cheeks. At Saturday evening dances, I would stand at the back of the hall, wearing my superior smirk and one of my sisters' inappropriately glamorous hand-me-downs—the black velvet evening dress with diamanté buttons, for instance; gold strappy high-heeled sandals; a gold bag to match. Feeling idiotic, poised between the terror of being approached by a boy and the excruciation of being overlooked, I would stand there, consumed with rage.

If anything kept my sense of myself alive

through those adolescent years—squashed as I was into my sisters' clothes like the least likely candidate for a drag show—it was my rage. I see now that it was the sort of rage that lends authority to—validates, really—the gender imperative of the male. Playing the wild young prince in a family of princesses carries with it a sense of dignity, of purpose. But, standing there, waiting to be chosen, I had lost all my power. I was ridiculous. And so, if a boy did finally approach me, if he uttered one cloddish comment, one idiot cliché, out would come a litany of savage phrases I always seemed to have at my command. And, for the moment, I would feel triumphant.

But only for the moment. As a woman, I was failing, that I knew. The standard female shriek-and-giggle mating dance was impossible for me. Apart from anything else, I talked too much. Verbal jousting was the only form of flirtation natural to me. I watched my sisters with dismay—the way they listened, rapt, when their men spoke; how they curled themselves into a chair, one leg over the other, caressing the stem of a sherry glass with manicured fingers. Such a performance, I knew, was impossible for me. I didn't even want to try.

It is one thing to eliminate the possibilities, however, quite another to find one's own way. Mine came as it always had — through defiance and self-assertion. But not before, at the age of nineteen, I went to a slimming salon and lost ten pounds. For the first time in my life, my cheekbones showed. With my stomach flattened out, my hips manageable, I began to feel at home in my body. I also began to feel at home with leg crossing and finger curling, neck stretching, shoulder twisting. And then, as I was sailing around the bottom of Africa on a ship to visit my sister in Cape Town, a young Italian math professor on his way home from Beira ventured to suggest that I looked quite different from what I actually was.

We were sitting in the ship's lounge, and I stole a glance at the mirror opposite. There I was in a shocking pink polka-dot dress and high-heeled sandals, my hair teased and sprayed, my eyes made up like birds' wings. We were the only young people on the ship — the Italian, his young sister, and I — and had quickly become friends, laughing, jousting, talking about jazz and books. I observed the sister carefully. She was appealing in her well-cut white cotton sundress and flat sandals, a touch of mascara, lip gloss, unvarnished nails. She had a loose, natural grace, not at all at odds with her wit and intelligence.

When I went back to my cabin that night, I sorted through my clothes, saving only a pair of shorts, one skirt, and a blouse. The rest I carried onto the deck and threw, piece by piece, overboard. That was the beginning. By the time I returned home a few weeks later, I had thought through how I now wanted to look.

I stopped teasing my hair, grew it long and straight, painted my eyelids black (without the wings), wore white lipstick, and smoked a cigar. My parents were highly entertained. Slowly, I collected a wardrobe of miniskirted shifts, shirts and ties, platform shoes, my first bikini. I chose

them in browns and blacks and whites, cor-
duroy, denim, cotton. Catching sight of myself
in a plate glass window now was like falling in
love, better than falling in love.

OVER THE YEARS, both on the page and off, I
have learned the same lesson again and again in
many different modes: I am no good out of character. My sense of male entitlement has carried
easily into every sphere of my life, even motherhood. When my own daughter longed for a
mother who wore wraparound skirts and loafers,
I laughed. After a while, she came to laugh, too.
She got quite used to a mother leaping onto the
roof to fix a gutter, dismissing fools with caustic
phrases. She herself struggled as quickly as she
could out of the corduroys and cottons I dressed
her in and into a wardrobe of flamboyant silks,
satins, and grosgrains that would have defied
even the imagination of my Pre-Raphaelite sister,
whom she closely resembles.

I, on the other hand, returning to South

Africa for visits, looked more than ever as if I had been borrowed from the neighbours. Standing there, all bone and beak, in a brown linen dress and wedged sandals, or khaki shorts and bare feet, I felt, each time, a version of the happiness that I had felt throwing my clothes off the ship.

Transformed from princesses into queens, my sisters still wore their startling primary colours and matching accessories. And I still clowned for my parents, to their delight. And if the books I wrote brought with them a certain measure of local notoriety—exposing the family to the scrutiny of the world—it was nothing more than they had all anticipated, one way or another all along. For my sisters, I was still a bit of a pest. For my parents, I had done what any chosen son could be expected to do: I had brought home what passed for glory, even if it was a little singed at the edges.

SEX WITH THE SERVANTS

THE FIRST LONG PIECE I EVER WROTE was an autobiography. It was an essay, written in my last year of school, in application for an American Field Service scholarship. Tell us about yourself, AFS said. And so I did. But, having no idea what to put in or leave out, I wrote down everything I could think of. I wrote ninety tedious pages, including details and characters apropos of nothing but the time and the place about which they were being written. (When I got to New York the following year, I was told that AFS had slapped a two-page limit on the biographical question. My essay had done it, they said.)

Twenty years and two novels later I returned to the same setting—Durban, South Africa—but, this time, I was writing a novel. It had taken me years to reach the point of even beginning such a novel. Not because scruples had held me back, but because the scenes and characters from my past were still chaotic, distorted by memory, without story or focus. Apart from this, I had been haunted by the awful curse of sentimentality and nostalgia. It had clouded the truth with threadbare images, useless abstractions.

I knew what I needed. I needed to cut through to the bone. But I just didn't know how. I had no proper voice yet for my subject. Nor had I come up with the proper object of revenge.

Revenge, for the purposes of fiction, concerns power. The power to expose, the power to

reorder, the power to understand. The word itself is cognate with *vindicate,* one of the meanings
of which is "to claim for oneself or as one's
rightful property." Revenge, in the broadest
sense, is the action generated by such a claim. It
is the power behind the impulse to write fiction,
and its objects lie within the writer. They teem
about, competing for attention. *Try me! Try me!*
But to find the proper object among the times
and scenes and characters which, potent as they
may be, are yet chaotic, distorted by memory,
without story or focus—this is the challenge
that a writer faces.

The proper object of revenge must be worthy. And, to be worthy, it must be either trouble
or love. Without the potency of one or the
other, there is no torque to discomfit the writer
into getting the fiction right, into setting herself
free so that the fiction can say again and again,
and always in the present: This is the way it is.

The process, if indeed it is a process—that
word so often invoked for the miserable struggle
of writing—has little to do with the petty

settling of scores. It goes, rather, to the heart of the pathology of the writer—to that moment that so many of us have forgotten in early childhood, when one came upon the pleasure of rearranging life with words. It has to do with justice itself, with the artist either as God or as mass murderer, whose driving force is to make things right in the world.

Like so many problems in writing, the problem I was having beginning this novel was solved by simply sitting down and writing— working and working with the words until, at last, I had the voice I wanted, a sentence, a paragraph. And, once I had the voice for the book, I began to understand the complex nature of the revenge I was dealing with.

The world I was writing about was the same world I had tackled for AFS, but now I could lift it from the restraints of myth and detail and report and do with it anything I pleased. Or, at least, so I thought. In fact, it seemed to twist itself out of my unconscious memory. Details, phrases, smells, and sounds flew back to me from God knows where. Objects shifted and changed and receded, myself among them. I began to feel the strangest sort of freedom.

I knew, as I wrote the novel, that I would be accused of writing autobiography. I have been accused of this in almost everything I have written. But to take heed of such accusations is to be paralyzed as a writer. And so I simply had to count on being understood by those I loved. Or, if misunderstood, on being forgiven. Or, if not forgiven, on not giving a damn.

Anyway, I was convinced that the novel would never be published. When I had finished three chapters, I sent them to my agent of the time. She wrote me back at length, two single-spaced pages. The family in my novel, she said, was exotic beyond belief. So was the setting. And why didn't I consider a linear family saga instead? "I'm not always sure I understand Ruth's violent or sadistic behavior," she wrote. She was referring, among other things, to a scene in the opening chapter, which I had set up in the opening paragraph:

> To a child, nothing that is familiar in her world—not earthquakes or revolutions, slavery or sodomy, poverty or riches—seems either exotic or wicked. So to me, Ruth Frank, white girl on a black continent, it felt only slightly odd to be diverting myself and my friend on an otherwise dull Sunday afternoon by pulling on the penis of the garden boy.

"The gardener's poor pants," wrote the agent—a transferred epithet if ever there was one. The coyness of the phrase—the distaste in her letter as a whole—stopped me dead. I considered my protagonist, her "violent or sadistic behavior." Did I understand it? Of course I did. I was that "violent or sadistic" child. I had grown up in a society of violent and sadistic children, had been schooled in the very crucible of genteel violence and sadism—a colonial version of a private British girls' school. But the fact is, I'm not sure that, given half a chance, all children the world over are not violent and sadistic—that the oppressive overlay of "niceness" in child-rearing America ("Be nice! Be nice!") isn't itself a player in a society seething with weapons and hatred.

Whatever the case, yes, I understood my protagonist's behaviour. But understanding is not the business of the writer—it is, rather, the benefit of having written. What the writer must know is how things happened, not why. I knew how. And I knew, too, that I did not want to write a linear family saga. Nor did I consider my material exotic. To me, despite the remove of time and distance, the world of which I was writing was so familiar as to be commonplace.

And so on I went. Over the next year, and in the spirit of defiance, I steered my protagonist and her family through sixteen more chapters. If a scruple came up, I thought, So what? The book will never be published anyway. Except for the two friends to whom I read what I was writing, I was gloriously free of audience. Never have I enjoyed writing anything as much.

Nor suffered nightmares quite so dreadful.

They were always the same: Me driving north across the Golden Gate Bridge with a paper bag on the passenger seat beside me. In the bag were the bones of five people. I had a fantastic story about chicken bones prepared for the toll collector (who was, somehow, taking tolls in the wrong direction), but he didn't give me a chance to tell it. "We know," he said, "what you've got in there."

Writers are natural murderers. Their murderousness is a form of sociopathy, fueled by resentment, scorn, glee, and deep affection. Before they can even begin writing, they must kill off parents, siblings, lovers, mentors, friends — anyone, in short, whose opinion might matter. If these people are left alive and allowed to take up residence in the front row of the audience, the writer will never be able to get the fiction right. More than this, she will never want to get it right. What she must do, if the fiction is to take breath, is to defictonalise the life, to disentangle it from the myths and fictions that we all create in order to control what we cannot alter. And then to work down, down, down, to the morally anaerobic heart of the matter within.

Little in this so-called process fits the modern idea of the writer-as-good-citizen — that midlist, pension-minded, smilingly affirmative, steadily productive, properly reviewed, ethnically overplayed, and, in the main, rather innocuous collegiate schlep, who very occasionally achieves the equivalent of a winning lottery ticket — a bestseller — and becomes a cultural icon.

The real writer, by contrast, is a moral reprobate. Words, in his psychic arsenal, are the closest thing he has to lethal weapons. If this is not the case, writing degenerates into a form of advertisement, and art itself is corrupted. So is the language. And so, by extension, is the culture.

No one, then, should doubt the wisdom of Joan Didion's warning that writers are always selling somebody out. Of course they are. Oh, they may smile and smile, and be fun to have around a dinner table. They might have friends, spotless married lives, successful children, and unresentful parents. But, in his study, on the page, the writer must, as Graham Greene said, have a sliver of ice in his heart. More than this even, he must have the heart of an assassin.

Ernest Hemingway, Truman Capote, Doris Lessing, Simone de Beauvoir, D. H. Lawrence, Edna O'Brien, Djuna Barnes, Henry Miller—these are only a few of the writers who would be in jail, or hanged, or banished, if they committed in life what they have done on the page: theft, libel, soul murder.

Which is not to say that the fiction itself must be without moral intention. Of course not. Think only of George Eliot taking on the role of an interested and analytical Jehovah, or of Jane Austen lacerating her hypocrites with irony. It is rather that the writer must be open—more than open, avid—for the surprise of truth, for the happiness, as William Maxwell put it, of getting it down right.

Where exactly does this happiness lie? It is hard to say—hard to fix the pleasure, the satisfaction, the comfort of getting life right on the page. Certainly, no small part of this lies in aesthetic happiness—the sight and the sound and the sense of the words themselves, the way they weave their effect, layer upon layer, giving shape and depth and color and tone to meaning: meaning to life, life in meaning.

And then there is the undoubted glee of exposure, the fun, the daring.

Reading Nancy Mitford's *Love in a Cold Climate* and *The Pursuit of Love*—novels based, like many of her others, on her own family—I am always enchanted by the fun and daring. Hers is a gloriously mad family—one that, I am sure, my old agent would have found even further beyond belief than my own. But what always strikes me anew each time I read her—what endears me yet again to that mad world of the Mitfords—is the sheer exuberant pleasure of the storytelling, the funniness of the characters themselves, their unquestionable authenticity.

> For months Nancy had sat giggling helplessly by the drawing-room fire ... while her thin pen flew along the lines of a child's exercise book. [says Jessica Mitford, in *Hons and Rebels*]. Sometimes she read bits aloud to us. "You can't publish that under your own name," my mother insisted, scandalized, for not only did thinly disguised aunts, uncles and family friends people the pages ... but there, larger than life-size, felicitously named "General Murgatroyd," was Farve. But Nancy did publish it under her own name, and the Burford Lending Library even arranged a special display in their window, with a hand-lettered sign: "Nancy Mitford, Local Authoress."

The helpless giggling, the flying pen—they precisely echo my own experience. Often, as I

her's story? How long would it have taken
n, if his father had lived on, to come to the
int of writing that novel?

One cannot know. But I would suggest that
e should never overlook two essential ele-
nts in the development of the writer: long
rs of practice and a ruthless determination to
ceed. Writers come to their material in dif-
ent ways, but come they must if they are to
ceed.

The role of ruthlessness itself—the sort of
hological ruthlessness that even the mildest
writers can reveal when having to choose be-
en truth and decency—this, I would say, is
nary. It involves not only the obvious inde-
cies, the revelation of bathroom habits and
ty adulteries, but, more than this, the revela-
n, through the story, through the characters
he story, of the human condition itself—its
ness, its absurdity, its loneliness, its familiar-
Is there a safe and decent way to accomplish
? I don't think so. If it is done right, some-
will be hurt.

wrote, I laughed aloud. I screamed with laugh-
ter—the entomologist skewering to the board
his prize beetles—those I adored and those I
despised, both. I forgot completely about the
parents who, still alive and in the present tense
at the other end of the world, kept asking me
what the new book was about. I didn't tell them;
I simply changed the subject. Except for the re-
curring nightmare about the chicken bones, I
don't remember worrying about them at all during those two years of furious writing.

Others, however, have had quite different
experiences from my own.

"If my father was alive," said V. S. Naipaul
about the writing of his novel *A House for Mr.
Biswas,* "clearly I wouldn't have been able to
write it. I wouldn't have wanted to do it. I probably wouldn't have even seen the material, the
way you don't see things in front of your
face. . . . I don't know whether his death wasn't
a kind of creative liberation for me. No one was
looking over my shoulder."

Marguerite Duras, writing in *The Lover* of her

own experience with autobiography—it was a novel that she wrote thirty-five years after publishing *The Sea Wall,* an earlier and very different novel written around the same characters—had this to say:

> I've written a good deal about the members of my family, but then they were still alive, my mother and brothers. And I skirted around them, skirted around all these things without really tackling them.
>
> The story of my life doesn't exist. Does not exist. There's never any centre to it. No path, no line. There are great spaces where you pretend there used to be someone, but it's not true, there was no one. The story of one small part of my youth I've already written, more or less—I mean, enough to give a glimpse of it. . . . What I am doing now is both different and the same. Before, I spoke of clear periods, those on which the light fell. Now I'm

talking about the hidden str
same youth, of certain f
events that I buried. I start
surroundings that drove m
Writing, for those people,
thing moral. Nowadays it
writing is nothing at all. Sor
ize that if writing isn't, a
founded, a quest for vanity
nothing.

Vanity and void—what I
addressing here is the pecul
heart of the writer's life—the
the self, gleaming on the page
time vanishing whole into th
words, both the exercise and
the ego—a process, I suppo
of psychoanalysis.

Still, what of her earlier
Naipaul's father? Of Naipau
his father alive, he could no

"Everything we write," said Adrienne Rich, "will be used against us, or against those we love."

"Everything you do is deliberately designed to cause your father and me as much hurt as possible," complained Doris Lessing's mother.

"When I wrote *Martha Quest*," wrote Lessing herself, "I was being a novelist and not a chronicler. But if the novel is not the literal truth, then it is true in atmosphere, feeling, more 'true' than this record."

In a battle of competing truths, fiction, if it is done right, will always win over what fondly passes for fact. Of course it will. It is life on the page. It has made order out of chaos, sense out of the senseless. It has given shape to lives that, without the intervention of the writer, had only the shape of chronology to them—that is to say, one long line.

"For what was the road I sought," wrote Italo Calvino, "if not a repeat of my father's, but dug out of the depths of another otherness, the upper world (or hell) of humanity, what were my eyes seeking in the dimly lit porches of the night . . . if not the half-open door, the cinema screen to pass through, the page to turn that leads into a world where all words and shapes become real, present, my own experience, no longer the echo of an echo of an echo."

In my own novel, for the sake of shape and form and plot, I gave the parents—who, like my own, were theatre people—a physical theatre, to which was attached a theatre school. In fact, my parents had never owned a theatre. Their productions were staged in a variety of local theatres, and my mother's theatre school was housed in an arts building in downtown Durban. Any writer knows how awkward it is to move characters in and out of rooms, let alone down a hill and through a race course to a theatre here, a theatre school there. Life is a mess; fiction is orderly.

Gabriel García Márquez once spoke of the difficulty he was having writing a novel that he had set in Cartagena. Cartagena is a walled city, and he was having enormous trouble moving his characters in and out of the several gates in the walls. One need only understand the difficulty of moving characters in and out of a *room* in fiction to appreciate this problem. But, in addition, he was having trouble with one of his characters, an old woman based on his own mother. She was by no means the main character in the fiction, but, whenever he put her into a scene, she took over. So, he knocked down the walls and killed off the mother.

This is what fiction can do. It can tidy things up; it can also rearrange the actual into what is commonly called "perceived reality." My own most dramatic instance of this occurred one evening, years after the novel in question, *Home Ground*, was published, when my mother, rather mellow on a glass of Scotch, turned to my father and said rather cozily, "Pity we had to sell the theatre, darling, isn't it?"

Jessica Mitford, describing a similar aftermath to Nancy's *Highland Fling*, wrote:

Thus Farve became—almost overnight—more a character of fiction than of real life, an almost legendary figure, even to us. In subsequent years Nancy continued to perfect the process of capturing him and imprisoning him between the covers of novels. . . . So successful was she that even the obituary writer of the *Times,* describing my father shortly after his death . . . betrayed a certain confusion. . . . As for Farve, he rather loved being General Murgatroyd. Now that he had been classified, so to speak, his Murgatroydish aspects began to lose some of their dread, even to take on some of the qualities of raw material for fiction.

Over time, the semiparasitic hold that fiction exerts on life seems to become stronger, the succession of fury and pride among the victims more complicated. Even those who have been left out may feel themselves overlooked. Telling them to give thanks doesn't help much. I suppose it is not very comforting to know that the party was lousy when you were judged unworthy of an invitation.

Most often, however, it is the skewered who are likely to object. And it is frequently the broader, more abstract betrayal that brings down on the head of the writer the lasting wrath of her victims. Write of a character's bat ears and he may laugh. Describe the vulgarity of his origins, his desperate need to redeem himself from same, and he will latch on to the bat ears and never forgive you. Nor will those who feel themselves to be uncomfortably close to the burning stake. Replacing the ears with a porcine nose or a profusion of nostril hair or a habit of conducting his dinner conversation with his fork will not diminish the broader affront, because the truth lies in the incontrovertible revelation itself—the life at the heart of that revelation. And this nothing cures.

Is it any surprise then, particularly at the outset, that the interested public will rail against a writer who holds up too bruising a mirror? Burn her books on the village green? Shun her in public places? Punish her family for having nurtured such a viper in the first place? And yet still, still there is a strong case to be made for taking on the living. Apart from the fact that it is braver to do so, it is also better for the art. Deaths, funerals, separations, divorces, bring out all sorts of unexpected lapses among survivors—lapses of memory, lapses into regret. And these can leave the writer with the awful legacy of sentiment and nostalgia, both of which make for very bad fiction.

FOUR YEARS BEFORE my father died and long before he fell ill, I wrote his funeral into my third novel. When the galleys came out, he and my mother happened to be staying with me in California, and he offered to vet them for me. I accepted gladly. My father was a detail man. Every letter from him was appended by a column of spelling errors I had committed in my own letter, entitled, "Yours." These were matched with another of his own, entitled, "Correct."

He sat at the dining-room table, turning the pages of my galleys, jotting down the corrections with care. And then, towards the end, he suddenly looked up with a very familiar expression of alarm. "Didn't give me much of a funeral, did you?" he said.

In fact, as I was writing that funeral, it did not occur to me to consider my father's extreme hypochondria, the way life in the family would come to a halt if he sustained a paper cut on his finger—Gentian violet, a carefully chosen plaster, and then the special chamois finger cots he kept for just such occasions, one for day and one for evening. I didn't think of that at all. But, even if I had, I would still have written that death, that funeral, weeping away as I did.

I AM ALWAYS intrigued when I encounter writers who claim to have chosen decency over truth—which is to say, they have chosen safety.

Or who, like Duras and Naipaul, say that they will not or cannot write about their parents/lovers/friends while those people are still alive. Unlike Duras and Naipaul—who, I am convinced, are exceptions in this matter—these other conscience-laden writers often seem to find, when the deaths do occur, that those absences do not actually bring the books behind them. More likely is the fact that the books would never have been written in the first place — that the writers lacked the necessary double vision, life and art—the necessary double morality as well.

ONCE MY OWN book, *Home Ground,* was finished and accepted for publication, the Golden Gate Bridge nightmare was replaced by the prospect of an actual visit from my parents. I told myself that they, too, were artists, that they would understand. We had, after all, grown up with the conundrum of living life as art. I felt sure they would grasp the artistic implications of transmuting life into fiction, that they would understand how one can simultaneously skewer one's characters on the page and still adore them in life. And that even if they didn't, they would forgive me. And yet—

Driving back from the airport, I tried to think that they were old and wouldn't want to plow through galleys on holiday, that they might take weeks to recover from jet lag anyway, by which time they would be ready to leave again for South Africa. But then, no sooner were they unpacked and down for tea, than they came to stand before me. "All right," they said. "Where is it?"

And so I was lost.

They read silently, hour after hour while I paced and cleaned things and stared out of the window, considering the serpent's tooth. And then, just as I was thinking that now, now they would give up and slam the pages to the floor and storm out of the house—just then they came into the kitchen and said, "Wonderful story! Can't wait to see the fuss it's going to cause at home! Ha! ha!"

It was one thing to be reprieved; quite another when the very people I had hoped would give fiction the benefit of the doubt began sizing it up as a weapon, taking revenge literally.

"Don't you think you were a little hard on Dad?" my mother said. "Although, between you and me, I think you were spot-on."

"She doesn't actually see herself in the book," my father complained. "You'd be doing me a great service if you'd simply point that out to her."

Then there were my sisters, to whom I had sent bound galleys. My middle sister, the harridan in the book, came up jubilant. "Now the world will know what it was really like!" she shouted across the airwaves. "But," she said, "I did not feed your rabbits dahlia leaves; I fed them avocado leaves." (She didn't; she was lying for a change.) From my other sister came praise too, and only one reservation, one request. "I think," she said, "that you could have been much harder on Ma and Dad. But do me a favor, old girl, don't put me in another book." (Trying to comply with the latter cost me about three years' work on my next novel. And then, finally, I did give up and put her into it, start to finish. "You have skinned her alive," a cousin told me after it came out. But my sister herself said nothing and never has. We remain abiding friends, with this great silence between us.)

With *Home Ground,* however, there didn't even seem to be a question of silence, of forgiveness. I flew off to South Africa with a very light heart for the launching of the book there.

What greeted me was a furor. SEX WITH THE SERVANTS! raged across the *South African Sunday Times* in a banner headline. There it was: columns of text and a loud, full-color picture of me — daughter of my parents, parent of my daughter — spread across two pages. "A novel describing a young white girl's trips into the servants' quarters to play sex games with a black gardener looks set to cause an outcry," the

article read. "Bound to shock conservative readers—it is expected there will be calls for it to be
banned."

I had been interviewed by the journalist who
wrote this in the offices of my London publisher. He was an old hand; I knew nothing. For
a good twenty minutes, he had us discussing
literature, the greats and smalls of it, my views of
Gordimer, Lessing, others. When he had me re-
laxed, he said, quite casually, "What do you think
the chances are of the book being banned?"

Well, I had never considered such a thing. I
had lived outside the country for sixteen years.
And anyway, politics was not the subject of my
story—it was part of the given, the ground, the
fabric of the world in which I had grown up.
When I had written that first paragraph, I had
known exactly what I was doing. I was choosing
an incident from childhood, not in shame or
guilt, but as deliciously riotous material through
which I could approach the riotous world in
which I grew up. The scene carried me right
back, not only to that world, but to myself in

that world. And, more than that, to myself as I wanted myself to have been in that world. To myself as Ruth Frank, the protagonist.

When the book came out, it was 1986, not 1953 (the date at which the novel begins). The mid-eighties were dark times for South Africa, times in which everyone seemed in a state of readiness for attack. Still, if the book were to be published now, I would expect the outcry to be every bit as loud, if in the opposite direction. I would expect to be accused of exploitation, of incorrectness, of not furthering the Cause.

"Great subjects," said V. S. Naipaul, "are illuminated best by small dramas." A young white girl's trip into the servants' quarters was my small drama. Colonialism, class disparity, race hostility, the enduring magnificence of Africa itself—these were the great subjects of my world. But I could no sooner have considered writing about them as such than I could have considered deep-sea diving or self-propelled flight. Nor could I have considered trying to further any causes. This is not the job of the fiction writer, nor should it be. "A cause," as Naipaul says, "always corrupts."

To my astonishment and dismay, the South African Broadcasting Corporation promptly canceled all my radio and television interviews. The newspapers followed suit. So did the universities. Only a bush radio station and some women's book clubs stuck to their guns and allowed me to speak.

And even then, I was brought down hard. Having been blessed by my own family's approval, I suffered miserably from the fury of strangers and near strangers. And I was absurdly surprised by it. Ridiculously, I felt myself betrayed. It didn't help when my parents—themselves, on occasion, the recipients of lousy reviews—tried to cheer me up by telling me that no man is a hero in his own country, that the only bad publicity is no publicity, etc. Clichés of comfort have never delivered much comfort to me.

And yet, in the end, they were right. Book

sales went far beyond the publisher's modest expectations. Whites, far and wide, were sending in for it, attracted by promises of interracial sex. So were many others. "Stir them up, girlie," beamed the Scottish woman who ran the local bookshop. "Stir them up!" The book went into a second and then a third printing. But still I was not comforted.

Day after day, I trekked off to address the book clubs. Women crowded into church halls and hotel auditoriums. Even those who wouldn't buy the book wanted to be able to come and sit in a group and nod together when one person asked, yet again, "Did that first 'situation' actually happen to you?" And then they would fold their arms and sit back while I tried to explain that the episode that seemed to have so incensed the country was being played out in variations under their own noses, in their own backyards. Didn't they realize, I asked, that they were setting me up as Galileo facing the Flat Earth Society? And then, when no one answered,

I moved into my favorite topic — the distinction between fiction and autobiography, between one sort of truth and another.

But as soon as the subject strayed from the garden boy's penis, the women began whispering to each other, unsnapping their handbags, and applying lipstick and powder. I would stop and ask whether there were any questions. And, always, someone raised a hand. "That episode with the garden boy—you don't mean to tell us that that happened to you?"

Few people attacked me directly. But I heard indirectly who was offended and why. Top of the list were white English-speaking middle-class liberals. They considered me a traitor to a multitude of their causes. Irresponsible for selecting their world to expose, frivolous for doing so with humor. I offended the Jewish community for the same reasons. I offended the old girls of my old school by writing about a lesbian headmistress. I offended an old lover by disparaging his so-called art and marrying him off to a woman he considered unworthy (my middle sister). I offended my brother-in-law exceedingly for the offense, as he put it, of disloyalty. And I offended my parents' admirers by writing about my parents.

People began to write and phone my parents from all over the country and the world. Some asked what had happened to me after Oxford. I had never been to Oxford. Some commiserated with them for having had to sell the house. "The house?" my mother barked. "But that was twenty-odd years ago!"

As I was about to leave South Africa, I went with my parents to say good-bye to an uncle. At his house we met one of the doyens of the local Jewish community (a man whom I took great glee in putting into my next novel). I had heard that this man disapproved of me and my book very much. When the subject came up, as it always did, he announced that he was a man who never read novels.

"Well, you should read hers," said my mother.

He read histories, he explained, biographies.

She pointed her considerable nose at him and lowered her lids.

But people had been talking, he said. His wife belonged to a book club.

I remembered his wife sitting in a group in one of my audiences. Someone had told me that she actually owned the book but had covered it in brown paper and read it while locked in the lavatory.

And now, he said, he had only one question to ask.

I knew what the question was.

"What question?" my mother demanded.

"Is the book autobiographical?"

"Stupid," said my mother. "What a stupid question!"

"No," I said. "It's not autobiographical."

He leaned back in his chair, triumphant. "So then why did you write it?" he demanded. "Can you answer me that?"

FALSE STARTS
AND CREATIVE FAILURE

SOON AFTER MY SECOND NOVEL, *Home Ground,* was published, my English agent delivered what turned out to be a near fatal injunction: "If you want to be taken seriously," he said, "we have to have another novel within a year."

The impact of such a statement changes one's life long before one understands the nature of its power. At the time, the words felt less like a threat than a sort of avuncular caveat. *Home Ground* was actually the third novel I'd written—the second was never published—each taking about two years to finish. So, I thought, I'll just do this one quickly.

Then he said, "What's the next novel about?"

I looked at him with the sort of blank stare of dreams: the exam book open on the desk and no idea how to proceed. This was far worse than "What books are you reading?"—a question to which I never seem able to conjure an answer on the spot. Caught by such a question, it is as if I am all at once revealed for the fraud I am—someone who puts herself to sleep at night with catalogues. As to the next novel, I was hard-pressed even to describe the novel that had just been published. What was it about? A girl growing up in South Africa in the fifties and sixties? I suppose so. A girl growing up in a theatrical family in the fifties and sixties? Yes, but not really. (Only much later did it dawn on me that the title of the novel itself, which I had had in advance of writing the first sentence, was the real subject of the book—of everything I'd written, in fact, and probably of everything I would ever write. *Home Ground.* It was a novel about belonging, about place and displacement. And if, as someone said, we have only one novel in us, I felt sure I had already written it.)

As to a new novel—well, I had no ideas. I had no need really, no real desire to write anything. Not for the moment. Not ever, perhaps.

"I think I'll write a sequel," I said.

He recrossed his legs and gave one of those smiling grimaces at which the English are so practised. "Oh no, no, no," he said, "not a sequel, please."

For some reason, publishers dislike sequels. Perhaps this is because, ideally, and in the absence of a bestseller, they want a string of first-novel attention for the books they sell. This being difficult to achieve for a published author who doesn't employ noms de plume, there is always the hope of a sort of a rising trajectory of new and different work to offer to the reading public, one example of which might fire that author into the light. I don't know. I have never got anywhere by trying to understand the publishing industry.

Whatever the case, when *Home Ground* was about to come out in New York, I had an almost identical conversation with my New York editor. "We need another book soon," she said. "It's been far too long since the last one." And then, "What's it to be?"

That was when the "what next" nightmare began.

Every time I start a novel or a story for which I am not ready, for which there is not the sort of frisson of conquest that comes with the foot placed surely on familiar territory, I have to learn again what I know already: fiction does not come out of ideas. The sources of fiction are myriad and complex—a character, a character in a situation, a phrase, a scene, a setting, a smell—anything at all but an idea attached to an intention.

When I sat down to begin the new novel—which, according to the English agent's schedule, should already have been in first draft—all that I had in the way of a beginning was a place. It was a bungalow situated on the northeast coast of South Africa, high above the Indian Ocean. I had gone there once as a girl in school. The place belonged to the family of one of the other girls in my class. They used it on weekends and for holidays. We were all taken out there one day on a bus, for a botany expedition to see a mangrove swamp near a lagoon. And then, afterwards, we were to have lunch on the verandah of the bungalow.

I have forgotten whose bungalow it was. I have forgotten everything about that trip but the gestalt of that wonderful dilapidated bungalow itself and the sight of the sea from its front verandah. Even then—although I did not grasp it as such at the time— there was the sure knowledge that this was an Africa more real than any I had experienced in my eleven or twelve years of growing up on that continent.

I didn't go back there again, and over the years—both before I left South Africa and during the many visits I have made there since leaving—I have driven past the area where I know the bungalow must have been. But I have never found it. There is no turnoff through the thick coastal bush, not even the hint of a driveway. I have walked the beaches around there too. Nothing.

In the end, it hasn't mattered. Another visit to the place could not possibly have made it more real than it had already become, and, quite possibly, it could have limited the usefulness by tying me down to specifics. I often find that a virgin visit, a purposeless visit, leaves one open to the magic of a place, if magic is to be found there at all.

The most majestic place to which I have ever been, for instance, is the Victoria Falls. They lie on the border between Zimbabwe and

Zambia, a place to which many South Africans used to travel. My family, however, did not. And so only after I had left the country did I first go there, during a visit home. Uprisings were happening in that part of the world then, something not incidental in my choosing to go: tourists were few, and I had the wonderful old Victoria Falls Hotel almost to myself. The first evening, I sat out on the verandah, listening to the thunder of the Falls. And then I went in to dine on crocodile drowning in white sauce and rosemary. The next morning, quite early, I walked off, through troops of baboons, to the cliffs and rain forest overlooking the Falls themselves.

Nothing I had ever heard or read about the place could have prepared me for that experience of looking down into that great roaring abyss, that cataclysm of waters with its arching, fractured rainbows, its mists and clouds rising into the air—the whole volume and force of the Zambesi plunging suddenly over a precipice more than a mile wide and 350 feet high into a deep and narrow gorge below. Standing on that slippery cliff in the warm, steady rain, with nothing between myself and such oblivion, I felt like the first person on earth, or the last.

I recount all this now to remind myself of how empty my second visit to the Falls was. I went back again a few years later to write a travel piece. What I had been asked to do was to try to reexperience the place, and to note down the sorts of details they needed — seasons and distances and bills of fare. But, with this brief, the magic of that first response was gone — that leap of the heart and the spirit, the wonderful sense of the world without myself in it. I stood where I had stood before. I admired; I recorded. And then I wrote the piece out of my first experience.

In just this way, the bungalow I had found as a girl, over all the years since I had first seen it, had become mine more surely in that first and only visit than it would have if I had returned and taken notes. More surely than if I had owned it myself.

How, after all, does one own such a place? How does one own any place? By buying it? By building on it? By happening to have grown up in it? No. And not by loving it, either. For the purposes of the imagination, one can only own such a place the way one owns one's own history: by experiencing it, by forgetting it, by re-creating it.

When I came to start the new novel, all I had to start it with was the re-creation of this bungalow and an idea for a character who had landed up there somehow, felt at home there for the first time in her life. Who she was, however, and why she had come there, I didn't know.

And that's when the nightmare began.

First I decided to give the bungalow to the protagonist's family and have her inherit it from her father. I called her Anna Diamond and wrote in the first person. The novel had no title. This is how it began:

> I stood at the edge of the verandah watching the sky blacken into an afternoon storm. The waves, coming in high with the late spring tide, roared out of sight two hundred feet below. The river too ran

strong for the time of year. Its dark water traced a cloud of brown almost a mile into the sea.

Well, this was all very well—I was fine as long as I was describing the bungalow. But, try as I might, I could not believe that Anna Diamond's was the sort of family who would own such a place. They were urban people, like my own family, people who would not venture out into the bush unless it were for a holiday at a game reserve or a resort. They were not really lovers of Africa either. Rather, they were temporary sojourners, there only for a few generations, with neither reason nor desire to own such a place.

That was the whole point: I needed a reason, I was mad to find a reason.

So, I came up with a mad sister, who had been banished to the bungalow with her nurse while she was growing up. I called the novel Winter in July, a play on the reversal of the seasons in the Southern Hemisphere. Here's how it began:

For the twenty years since my sister Josephine left, the bungalow had stood empty. But now, with my father's death, it was mine. And still it seemed beyond the reach of normal life and rules.

I stood at the edge of the verandah watching the sky blacken into an afternoon storm. The waves, coming in high . . .

But soon I found myself wound up in the sister's madness, explaining and explaining in order to give authenticity to a place that was proving fairly intractable. It kept shrugging off my pathetic attempts to colonise it. And anyway, it wasn't a novel about a mad person; it was a novel about a woman called Anna Diamond, who had come back to South Africa and had landed up, somehow—although not this how— at the bungalow. The bungalow stood; the story faltered.

I tried her in the third person.

"Anna Diamond stood at the edge of the ve-randah, watching the African sky blacken into an afternoon storm. The waves, coming in high," etc.

Fine as far as it went. But first person/third person was not the problem. As soon as I tried to move the story on from the bungalow, I dried up. I became convinced that until I solved this very basic problem—who was in the bungalow and why—I couldn't go on. (In fact, I couldn't. Fiction has an odd way of both failing the tentative and resisting hot pursuit. Imposing solutions falls under the latter category.)

So I decided to bring Anna Diamond back to South Africa from the United States and place her boldly in the bungalow, to hell with it:

> The first real choice Anna Diamond ever made was to return to Africa. She made the choice alone. She made it unconditionally. And she made it against the advice of everyone she knew . . .
>
> [She] stood at the edge of the verandah, watching the African sky blacken into

an afternoon storm. The waves, coming in high . . .

All very well, there she was. I went on with this for a chapter or two, and even gave them as readings on occasion. This was a mistake. People would come up to me afterwards and say, "When will the book be out?" "Dying to know what happens."

Well, so was I. But I knew enough not to say so. Those questions, however natural and welcome they might have been once the book was actually written, simply gave voice and substance to the torment I was in.

What was this novel actually about? However much I wrote and rewrote the opening descriptions of the bungalow—the writing itself was never the problem with this novel, the writing itself seldom is—however sure-footed I may have felt about the place, I was timid with the story, with the characters. I didn't know this woman; I didn't know the people she had come back to. Worse still, I couldn't want to write her story. "Who cares?" I kept asking myself—a deadly question in fiction. The answer was— the answer always is when one has to ask it—No one.

The only comfort I could take was in reading of the trials of other writers.

"I type out beginnings and they're awful," says Philip Roth. "I need something driving down the center of a book, a magnet to draw everything to it."

"One must have blind faith [to write]," said Jean Rhys, "like walking on water. . . . I must have been crazy when I thought it would be easy. . . . One false start after another."

"I would wish to believe," said Frank O'Connor, "that, if you work hard at a story over a period of twenty-five or thirty years, there is a reasonable chance that, at last, you will get it right."

Comforted or not, as soon as I got back to my novel, I was stupid again. Desperate, too. I kept changing the title. The right title, I hoped, might pull the story behind it. Here is what I came up with:

Foreign Territory; In a Foreign Land; Resident Alien; Close to Home; Stranger in a Strange Land; Some Time Overseas; Equal Strangers; Time and Distance; A Way of Life; Voluntary Exile; Far from Home; Overseas Visitor.

Of course, it was hopeless. Still, I chased on. I thought that if only I had the idea for the story, I'd have the novel itself. I forgot everything I knew about ideas and fiction. But desperation and vanity does this to a writer: it makes her stupid. In fact, finding an idea for a novel is easy. I came up with one idea after another. In this case, coming up with an idea for the book was almost a guarantee that whatever I wrote to fit that idea would falter. The more obsessed I became with chasing down a plan, with wrestling the novel into the confines of an abstraction, the more the real fiction eluded me. Nancy Willard once wrote, "A writer with a fixed idea is like a goose laying a stone." I was that goose; I was a gaggle of such geese.

In the end, I am not sure that it really matters how literary authenticity is achieved. The territory of fiction—that mysteriously achieved world created by the workings of the imagination—seems most often accessible only through a more or less infuriating struggle with creative failure.

Several times, I threw the book out and decided that that was it, I would not willingly and knowingly play Sisyphus with fiction. I would write essays; I would write short stories. To hell with agents and editors. I had written forty pages in two years and hadn't got beyond a woman standing on the verandah of a bungalow, looking out over the sea. I'd leave her behind.

But I've never been good at putting failures behind me, certainly not half-baked ones. I am too compulsive, too tidy. To abandon hope for an unpublished novel—such as my second, which I'd written off—this is not the same as abandoning a novel that has yet to take shape, and that, somehow, feels as if there's a shape it could take if only you could find it. The problem was that my imagination, or what was left of it after the battery of intention and ambition, was in revolt. Or in retreat. Anyway, it had left home.

At about this time, I read a review, written by Madeleine L'Engle, in which she reported saying to her students, "Don't think. Write. We think before we write a story, and afterward, but during the writing we listen."

This was exactly the problem I was having. I had deafened myself with thinking. The way I write best is in scenes, scenes built upon scenes. But, in this novel, the scenes didn't tie together. My protagonist didn't belong where I had put her. And, anyway, who was she? I had no idea. Under the weight of my anxiety, the novel would no sooner struggle to the surface than it would sink, surface, then sink. There was nothing below the water to hold it up, no seven-eighths of the iceberg. I knew that, but I didn't know how to solve the problem.

"What I want to feel," said Somerset Maugham, "is that it's not a story I'm reading, but a life I'm living." One can as easily apply this to the writing of a story. To get the story right, one must feel that one is living a life rather than writing it. And this is precisely what I could not do.

The question I ask myself now is, What should I have done? Should I have let the thing marinate, as I have so often advised others to do, or should I have pushed on, as I did, through four or five miserable years, trying to get it right? I don't know; I can't know.

But I did push on. My protagonist returned to teach for a semester at the university. Then she returned to look after her mad sister. Her name changed from Anna Diamond to Joanna Stern. The novel was now called Halfway to India.

"Joanna Stern stood at the edge of the verandah watching the sky blacken into an afternoon storm. The waves, coming in high with the late spring tide," etc.

I could have known that changing a name changes nothing. Nor does changing a title if the fiction isn't there to start with. Still, I changed

the title to Equal Distance and then to Pride of
Place. The fact is, fiction hasn't a chance to
breathe under the weight of publishing anxieties,
or life anxieties. It should ride them out, not
carry them on its back.

Sometime in the middle of this awful period,
I had a dream, which I wrote down:

> I went to live with an elephant, a rather
> fractious one. I made clothes for it. At first
> its trainer, who was a sort of concierge,
> thought I wouldn't be able to handle the
> animal. But, in fact, the elephant and I be-
> came quite fond of each other, used to
> each other. The place in which the ele-
> phant lived was a castle, or a prison on top
> of a mountain, and shaped like an ele-
> phant's quarters in the zoo. No one else
> could handle this elephant, but the keeper
> seemed to assume I could.

The dream wasn't difficult to work out. In itself, it told me nothing that I did not know. But,

having had it, a wonderful thing happened. I gave up. So did my agents, so did my editors. They assumed I was a one-book author (the first book didn't count; it hadn't been noticed enough). Not that they had been nagging me for the book—they hadn't—but I had felt the weight of expectation in questions like, "How's the novel going?" "Anything to show me?" All that stopped.

I decided to write magazine pieces, to do a bit of travelling. I went to the Middle East, down the Nile, through southern Africa and South America. I sold a house and bought a house. The sky didn't fall in. I might have been a bit lonely without a novel to write, but loneliness, as Rilke pointed out, "is very good practice for eternity."

And then, one summer, I was invited by the Rockefeller Foundation to spend five weeks at the Bellagio Study Center on Lake Como. In my proposal I had written four words: "A book of fiction." And now here was the challenge again: make good, come through, try again.

My room and study at the Villa Serbelloni looked out over beautiful terraced gardens and vineyards, over the church towers and terracotta houses of Bellagio, and then, beyond that, over Lake Como itself. I had French doors leading out onto a little balcony, a glass-topped desk with a ream of 100 percent rag bond, beautiful pens and pencils, a pencil sharpener, an eraser, a notebook—all new, all wonderfully Italian. But where was the computer I'd been told would be mine for the visit? I went downstairs to enquire of the director.

There'd been a hitch, he said. In his charming Mediterranean way, he told me that someone's spouse had wanted a computer, and now it seemed that she would be using it until she left, another two weeks. Meanwhile, I could print out whatever I wished from my disks on the foundation's computer; I could write in the notebook, would that help?

I decided to take a walk down to the lake for coffee, three hundred–odd steps down, a double espresso and a look in the shops, three hundred steps up again. By the time I was back in my study, the panic was manageable. I sat down. I took up one of the pencils, opened the notebook, and wrote, "Untitled." Then I had to lie down on the bed and sleep for the rest of the day.

I'd written my first two novels with pencil and paper, written them in a flash through one draft; typed it out, cut and pasted, and rewritten. But now the ease of editing-as-you-go on a computer had changed my way of working completely. I tried hard to remember how I'd done it.

After breakfast the next morning, I printed out the twenty-five false drafts I had on my disk, took them back up to my study and read them through. I also read through the file of notes I'd brought. And then I put them all in an envelope and put them away in my suitcase. I opened the notebook, underlined "Untitled," and began to write.

I like to think that the pencil and paper themselves — the simple, laborious, almost nostalgic act of fashioning words by hand — were responsible for the ease with which I now wrote. As I was writing the new opening, I even seemed to be hearing the words differently, fake from real. Hearing the story too. And, once I did, I knew quite clearly who my protagonist was. What was all the fuss about? My Anna Diamond, my Joanna Stern—my many-named, variously described protagonist, with her disparate reasons for inhabiting a bungalow on the coast of southern Africa—was really Ruth Frank, the narrator of *Home Ground,* grown up now and sobered. And whatever the editors said they didn't want from me, what I wanted was to write a sequel. And that was what I was doing.

From that point on, I had no trouble with the novel. I knew my character and I knew why she had come back. She had come back to attend the apparent death of a parent, and she would go to the bungalow, certainly, but it wouldn't be her bungalow at all. It would belong to her first lover, a lover whom she had left behind eleven years before and with whom she would take up again. The lover, Hugh Stillington, would come from the sort of family from which some of the girls in my class at school had come — colonial money, land money, sugar money.

With this I felt at home. I wrote on. I moved the novel from the 40 pages with which I had been obsessing — and which I had now rewritten entirely — to 100, 250, 350. This is not to say that the process was easy — I'd be stuck here or there, of course, and think, This is it, here I go again — but in the main I knew what I was doing. The territory was my own, its characters, its story. It was a novel about place and displacement: *plus ça change, plus c'est la même chose . . .*

The day I finished the novel, I still didn't have a title. None of the titles I had used seemed right. I had put them in and taken them out one after another until I started writing properly. And then I forgot about a title and all the superstitions that go along with it. But now I had finished; I needed one.

A friend was coming for dinner, and I asked her for suggestions.

"But what's it about?" she said.

I told her. I gave her the manuscript. She opened it here, opened it there at random.

"What is this bungalow?" she asked.

I told her.

"So, call it The Bungalow," she said.

And there it was, a title low on cleverness. I sent the manuscript to my New York editor. She gave me some notes for a rewrite — leave out one of the sisters, she said, a few of the scenes, and, by the way, you have far too many dogs in this novel. I cut out the sister (a big mistake, as it turned out) and put a few more dogs in for good measure. And then, on a trip to New York, I delivered the final manuscript myself. The publisher called me in a few days later. "Lynn," he said, "you have thrown away a big novel here. You have a black man murdering a white man — why didn't you put it up front?"

"But that's not at all what the novel is about," I said, completely surprised.

"What is it about then?" he asked.

I gave him the place and displacement speech. He looked skeptical. "Put the murder up front," he said, "and we'll publish it."

It was a deal. And away I went to write a new beginning. I didn't mind in the least. I knew I could write a new scene for the front of the book without changing the nature or the point of the novel. In fact, I could use the scene to tie things up, front and back. And I could still have my protagonist standing on that bloody verandah, looking out at the sea—which now came later anyway—using all my old phrases and images, polished to a gloss over five years of rewriting. The point was that I knew why she was there: I had written the book.

EMBRACING THE ALIEN

IT TOOK ME FIFTEEN YEARS IN AMERICA
to find the perspective from which to write
about South Africa. Despite what I had lived
and seen and known there, I couldn't seem to
break out of a sort of public way of seeing the
place, and, therefore, a public way of knowing it,
of writing about it too.

So much writing begins—and fails—in such a public arena. One notices only the obvious, tries out the well-worn approach, the predictable angle, the same old voice for the piece at hand, only to have it emerge predictable and same—flat, dull, lifeless. What to do? How to conquer one's natural sloth and go after a truth that has nothing to do with perceived expectation?

To those who haven't tried it, writing the truth seems like a simple thing to do: you see it, you know it, you write it down. But to reach the simple truth on the page—and it is always simple, for all its complexities and contradictions—takes a particular way of seeing and, therefore, a particular way of knowing. It concerns the language of seeing and knowing. Above all, it concerns the transmutation of experience through language into life on the page.

For the young expat South African writer of the seventies and eighties, the perceived audience for her writing fell loosely between what

I call the Out-of-Africa crowd on the one hand—wildlife, gorgeous scenery, exotic native peoples—and the Keepers of the Moral High Ground on the other. In the first category there was no problem: life in South Africa seemed to translate as exotic whatever one did with it. It was the moral high ground crowd that gave trouble. They seemed to dictate the terms and draw the margins, leaving hardly any space to move or breathe.

And so, for a number of years, I occupied myself writing predictably horrified short stories placed in South Africa. They were full of fake daring, fake feeling, fake everything. And they were, of course, predictably rejected. The reason was obvious. The subject matter was public property; I could not find a way to make it my own because it was not my own. And so the stories sank under their own dead weight. The more I tried, the stupider they became. The page will reveal the fake even when the writer is moving herself to tears. "Only that which does not teach," said Yeats, "which does not cry out, which does not persuade, which does not condescend, which does not explain, is irresistible."

Writers seem to suffer more than most in wanting to be loved, or, perhaps, in wanting to be admired (which, I suppose, amounts to the same thing). At least they want this until they discover that the only way truly to be loved and/or admired is to find their own way, forgetting the audience. Longing for an audience and therefore guaranteeing none is, perhaps, the greatest curse of the writer.

Which brings me back to my own situation. The only thing for me to do was to leave the world of South Africa alone until I could find another way of writing my way into it, a way that would not leave me writhing in embarrassment. Failing that, I proceeded to write two novels with an American cast of characters, using the rather sardonic voice of a seventies middle-class woman embracing defiance. I lived with this voice the way one lives with the wrong sort of man—year after year after year.

Oddly enough, the first time I fell into a voice with which I was completely comfortable was in a short story that I placed in America. At the age of eighteen, I had come to the United States as an American Field Service exchange student. On the assumption that I, having come from a Jewish family, would feel most at home with a Jewish family, AFS placed me in Far Rockaway, New York, where I lasted for about six weeks. (I was then moved to a gentile family in Greenwich, Connecticut, where I was much happier and stayed out the year).

Years later, back in America as a graduate student, I began to tell my American friends about the Far Rockaway experience, about the trips to the bowling alley, the trips to the Catskills, the trips to the wholesale houses of the Lower East Side. Over time, the whole experience became a mine of entertainment, the stories polished and refined to a gloss. (What I left out, because it didn't fit the stories as told, was the extent of my homesickness and misery during those six weeks—the way I slept twelve to fourteen hours a day and couldn't eat and lost twenty pounds and read all six Jane Austen novels over and over, like an addict.)

As with so much in the writing of fiction, there was immense comfort for me in the telling of these stories, the comfort of laying a ghost. With the safety of distance and time, I found I could control the experience by transmuting it into a manageable shape, a shape it had never really had. Using irony and timing, creating scenes that distilled rather than reproduced what had actually happened, developing character through dialogue that never took place, I somehow solved the experience as story.

But every time I tried to *write* the story, it fell flat. I could no longer rely on mimicry and gesture or on the sort of timing that is created by the idiosyncrasies of a particular audience at a particular time. I kept starting too soon, filling in too much background.

And then, one day, considering the fact that I, a Jew, had been placed by gentiles in a family of American Jews on the assumption that we would all get along swimmingly, I landed on a biting opening paragraph:

> I was once told by a displaced Rumanian, fellow Jew, in a variation on the old adage, that each country gets the Jews that it deserves. What was I to make, in the light of this, of my first day in Far Rockaway, New York, with the family Grossman? I knew already that all Jews were not the same. But what, I wondered, did America do to deserve this?

This sort of bad behaviour has always appealed to me. It seems to loosen my tongue, sharpen my teeth. Gleefully, I moved through the Far Rockaway story, and, as I did, found it taking on a shape quite different from the one I had told to others. It was also quite different from the one that I had lived through myself. I bit into the subject and shook it and shook it until I had shaken the truth out of it.

And then there it was, about forty-five pages

of it. I packed it up and took it along to the only writing workshop I have ever attended. During the first session, which happened to be on opening paragraphs, I read out my own. The writer conducting the workshop asked if she might see the whole story, and then, once she had read it, she asked whether she might edit it down for use in a craft class she had to teach.

I could not have been more delighted. Seeing how she managed to reduced the story to twenty-two tight pages, cutting and pasting, working transitions, removing all the carefully provided background information and thereby giving shape and form and thrust to the story itself—well, this was the best education I could have asked for. When I returned to California, I began to submit her version of it.

And back it came, mostly with slips, but occasionally with one of those cheerful "Try us again!" notes attached. And then one magazine editor suggested that the opening paragraph itself was the problem. As is, it was unpublishable, he said. Perhaps I should consider changing it and then resubmitting.

Well no, I wouldn't. Apart from anything else, it was easy to refuse such a request in the face of no guarantee of publication. But I think now that it would have been easy to refuse anyway. The opening paragraph was the hook of my story. More than this, it was the paragraph in which I had fallen into a voice both new and, at the same time, completely familiar to me. It had taken me back to myself as a child, perhaps, to the sort of provocative behaviour practised at the far end of the dining-room table. Whatever the case, it had brought with it a new and completely familiar way of considering the world—a way of seeing, a way of knowing, that I had never before been able to translate onto the page.

(Some years later, the story was included in an anthology of Jewish women writers, published by the venerable Jewish Publication Society. The opening paragraph was never mentioned before or after publication.)

The other great service that the workshop teacher had performed for me was to ask me, one evening over dinner, what my first novel was about (it was then in galleys). When I told her—when I went on to talk of the second novel that I had just finished (a novel which has never been published), all those women liberating themselves in predictable ways—she pulled a face. "For God's sake," she said, "why aren't you writing about your own family?"

Well, why not? Perhaps one only hears such a question when one is ready to answer it. Having long since given up my bid for the approval of the moral high ground crowd, I was still nowhere near finding a way into the story of my own family, my own world. Whenever I had tried, the story had come off as a cartoon of itself, often sentimental, with no life, no truth on the page. Now, however, with the voice I had found in writing "Foreign Student"—and with what seemed like the ideal audience posing the question—I went home and immediately sat down to write the first paragraph of my third novel, *Home Ground.* It was easy after all.

The novel tells the story of a girl who, like me, had grown up in South Africa; whose family, like mine, were Jewish; whose parents were actors, as mine were; and who spent much of her childhood, as I had, dreaming of escape into the "real world."

Such dreams were common among South African children, then as now. Apart from the remoteness of the country itself, its colonial history had always pointed north, usually to England. As a new university graduate with a scholarship to study overseas, I, too, would probably have gone to England (and probably been just as homesick there). But I was not: I was off to America to go to graduate school, and, not incidentally, to consider marrying a man I hardly knew, a South African who was living there. It seemed like a delightfully mad thing to do — so far, so foreign, so reckless.

In fact, there was nothing mad in it. It was a clear-eyed bid for a chance at the life I had always wanted and never known how to obtain. But this was almost as hidden from me as it was from my parents. We all understood, although tacitly, that, scholarship or no scholarship, they could never have afforded an overseas education for me; that I was involved in a troublesome affair with an inappropriate man at home; and that, short of marriage, I would have to find my own way in the world somehow. If America had presented itself yet again—it had been over two years since I had returned from AFS—well, that was where I should feel mad enough to go.

To the quasi-colonial in the sixties, America was never a serious choice as a place to live. With British hauteur towards all things American, South Africans considered America too young, too unbaked, a country that did not take itself seriously. America was a cartoon life, a comic life—people hitting each other over the head with frying pans, people falling out of windows and bouncing back up. As for a serious education there—impossible. Oxford and Cambridge were the traditional goals of the serious

South African student. Attending graduate school in New York, as I was to do, seemed frivolous, illegitimate. English literature in America? Ridiculous!

Still, there I was. And there we were, my new husband and I, on the corner of 112th and Broadway. The building itself was quite standard for married-student housing, the apartments well-furnished and air-conditioned. At twenty-one, I was rather delighted with the idea of what I had done, and with the pots and pans and sheets and towels of this strange new life. It felt like playing at real life — making meals, making beds, making love.

And yet, within weeks of moving in, I slipped into what I now recognise as a form of shock. I dressed, I attended classes, I made new friends. But nothing I did seemed connected to anything that had gone before or to what might follow. In the urban cacophony in which I lived, my spirit seemed sunk in silence — deep and wide and terrifying.

New York alone had not done this. Nor had

the homesickness from which I was suffering again so acutely. The problem was of more existential proportions. It went something like this: If nobody knows me, who am I? If nothing is familiar, where am I? And, if I don't want to be here, why am I?

Twenty years later, long out of the crisis and living in California, I wrote in my journal: "I do not belong here, and I have had to turn not belonging into triumph." The triumph, such as it was, was modest. I had degrees. I was teaching. I had written three novels and published two. And I was working on a fourth, a sequel to *Home Ground* called *The Bungalow*.

It was only in the writing of this new novel that I began at last really to understand those first years as a graduate student in America. The novel takes place in 1975. Ruth Frank, my protagonist, now an adult and living in America, returns to South Africa to visit her aging parents. Wound into the novel, in flashback, are scenes from Ruth's life in America, starting at the beginning, in the late sixties in New York, a time and a circumstance very like my own.

George Bernard Shaw once referred to England and America as two countries separated by the same language (Oscar Wilde produced a variation on this, and so did Dylan Thomas). As I wrote on in *The Bungalow,* I remembered how much more severe the paradox of that barrier had seemed during those first years in America, dividing my life here from there, present from past. Language itself is only one aspect of the extended vernacular of a culture. There is also the timing, the rhythm, the sights and smells and sounds of daily life. Putting on a winter coat, facing into the icy wind off the Hudson, crossing the street to avoid the madwoman screaming obscenities at the corner of 113th, stopping at Chock full o' Nuts for coffee and a donut, and then having to stand at a high table to eat because no seats were provided by the establishment—well, I felt every bit as foreign as the Cambodian graduate students who lived in the apartment next door.

I grew up in the middle of a sizable city, in a large Anglo-Jewish, quasi-Bohemian, quasi-Victorian household of family and servants and dogs. There was also an enormous extended family, including grandparents, aunts, uncles, and twenty-seven first cousins. My sisters and I were sent to a very British Anglican girls' school, where there were very few Jewish girls and where we sang hymns and said Christian prayers every morning. And then, three afternoons a week, we went to Hebrew school with other Jewish children. At night, when most parents were home from work, ours went off to rehearsal or to a performance. Every Friday night and on Jewish holidays, we gathered for dinner with one or the other side of the family— twenty, thirty, forty, of us sometimes. Our lives were noisy with family, with theatre parties, with performances, and with our own private family dramas.

In America, by contrast, there was only my husband and I—no standards but what we might set ourselves, no familiar rituals, no duties, no audience for our lives. Although he and I had come from quite different sorts of families, with different educations, different social sets, different manners, different everything, we were more alike in America than we would ever have been at home. And even then, he was the one who felt more at home in this strange new society.

In his brilliant novella, "One Out of Many," V. S. Naipaul tells the story of a servant in Bombay who comes to Washington with his employer. In Washington, Santosh, the servant, discovers the immigrant's truth: stay away long enough, and you belong nowhere anymore. "One day," says the narrator, "I found I no longer knew whether I wanted to go back to Bombay. Up there, in the apartment, I no longer knew what I wanted to do." And then, in the profoundly sad finale, he comes to the conclusion: "I was once part of the flow, never thinking of myself as a presence. Then I looked in the mirror and decided to be free."

Naipaul himself has said in an interview, "Leaving home was an immensity. I've been trying all my life to express that, the bigness of that. The central experience of my life."

He is not alone in this. I think of Katherine Anne Porter saying, "The summer of my Texas childhood forms the only living background of what I'm trying to tell." And of Carson Mc-Cullers saying, "I must go home periodically to renew my sense of horror."

"So primary is homesickness as a motive for writing fiction," says Joyce Carol Oates, "so powerful the yearning to memorialize what we've lived, inhabited, been hurt by and loved, that the impulse often goes unacknowledged."

"*Lacrima rerum,* the tears of things, the tears in things," said Naipaul, on being suddenly reacquainted with *A House for Mr. Biswas* twenty years after he wrote it. "My literary ambition had grown out of my early life; the two were intertwined; the tears were for a double innocence."

Leaving home is perhaps the central experience of the writer's life regardless of whether he or she ever returns. In a broader sense, being out of the society of home provides the remove at which the writer must live in order to see, in order to write. It is this enigma that informs the writer's perspective—the restless pursuit of a way back while remaining steadfastly at a distance.

I HAVE ALWAYS been a natural foreigner: there, here, anywhere. From an early age, my fantasies centered themselves around a restless vision—a vision of a life lived between two worlds—someone just arrived, just about to leave, and always with somewhere to go home to.

Living in America had given me this distance. It had also given me the benefit of the doubt as a professional expatriate on a number of other fronts. America is kind to expatriates, particularly to those who have what passes for a British accent. Confronting daily the anomaly of my presence in a country that was both my home and could never be home to me, I found it easy to contemplate the conundrum of alienation and belonging. Alienation became my subject. In fact, it was my subject long before I even left home.

I think of this when I have to account, yet again, for the fact that I have lived so long in America and yet can never seem comfortably to place my fiction in it. With anything but a foreign perspective, I lose my boldness. I watch my step, I worry about getting things wrong. Once, after trying and failing to place a short story on American soil, I just let it slip offshore, and there I could settle in quite nicely onto an island.

After *Home Ground* was published, I began to write articles on South Africa, always from the perspective of someone who had left. I wrote about revisiting the house in which I had grown up, about revisiting the country both before and after Mandela was set free. I wrote a short story about a young Zulu woman leaving home to go and seek work in the city. I wrote a story and then a novel about a young Englishwoman who leaves home to go to South Africa and make her way there. The subject of leaving home seemed to have no bottom to it.

Why then did I not simply return to South Africa? one may reasonably ask. Why leave the place and the people that I loved only in order to be able to return for a few weeks a year? Even though I pretended to ask myself this question, the answer did not really interest me. Or, rather, the answer seemed to lie in an impulse that was as familiar to me as the rhythms of my breathing. It involved not only the foolishness of reclaiming a future in a country mired in political mayhem, but, even more than this, in giving up the chances of a future in the real world. Of giving up choice.

I was not alone in this. Among my expatriate South African friends, the phenomenon of longing for home while staying steadfastly away from it was a given. Bring expatriate South Africans together, serve them a strong curry, biltong, boerewors, melktert, koeksusters, and, sooner or later, you will have a maudlin crowd, a crowd mourning lost paradise. Or a crowd laughing at the funniness of life in America.

Apart from the odd South African expat, my main connection between the two worlds in which I now lived were the letters my mother wrote me every day, the letters I wrote back. I told my parents what they wanted to hear— real-world things—the opera, the plays, the star performers I had seen, the essays I was writing, exams I had taken, honours, degrees, publications. But, above all, I told them how happy I was. Writing those letters seemed to make sense of having left in the first place, and of my life in America through the decades of longing to go back, all those many years of reported happiness.

There is an odd phenomenon in place among certain South Africans. It is the discouragement, loud and clear, that comes in the face of any suggestion of return. The reasoning behind this is fairly simple: if one person can leave and thrive, then the chances of others being able to do so are higher. By the same token, if an ex-patriate returns, immense failure is implied, not only for oneself, but for all those looking to en-sure their futures in the real world.

What is being played out here involves a colonial brand of ambition that speaks to the phrase so often twinned with "real world"— "making it." Making it in the real world is not something to be given up lightly, certainly not to return to a country as politically fraught as the South Africa of the seventies and eighties, or even to the South Africa as violent as it is today.

And so, what I could not tell my parents in the letters I wrote—what I hardly understood myself yet—was the scope and range of the loneliness in my new life. The cost of the bar-gain in which we had all tacitly taken part.

Once, after a few years in America, I did suggest to my mother that we were considering coming back. "Oh no!" she cried. "It's too soon! Why not go to London? London is the hub! That's where you really belong!"

Perhaps it was then that I began to understand my responsibility for sustaining the triumph of my departure. If I went back, I would have to rewrite not only my place in the family, but my own future as well. It was unimaginable.

There is an odd lag between playing the life and writing around it. By the time I was writing *The Bungalow,* the longing to return to South Africa had died down. I was reconciled. More than reconciled, I had begun to understand that it was no accident that I had chosen to stay on in America. In America, I could play myself, free of the sort of colonial categorising that I would have had to overcome in England (a South African, a Jewish South African). In addition, I now had American friends, an American child. I was an expatriate, living in America. And that is where I would remain.

I have never understood the concept of assimilation, not for myself anyway. How would I disappear into America? And why would I want to? As a writer, I need the specifics, I need the differences. I also need the distance at which I keep myself from my subject, from my life, past and present. And I have always needed this. If I have learned the language of life in America, if I have made friends here and found in them a generous audience for the performance of my life, then this is what I have become, what I have always been, in fact: a performer of myself.

Just after finishing *The Bungalow*, I went out to South Africa, accompanied by two American friends. In my twenty-five years in America, this was the first time I had taken anyone other than my daughter home with me. When we were in Durban, I took my friends to see the house in which I had grown up, where my father had grown up before me—a colonial, pillared splendour, commanding a ridge high above the city. It is the house of my imagination, a house that I have inhabited again and again in my fiction. As we stood on the upstairs verandah, looking out over the city and the bay, the Indian Ocean beyond, one friend turned to me and said, "How could you bear to leave this place?"

I stared at her. No one had ever asked me

this before. And yet, of course, it was a question I had been asking myself all my life. Being asked it now, though, and by a dear and intimate friend, brought the whole issue back de novo, all the deep and suspect sadness of my self-imposed exile.

And then, all at once, standing there on the old verandah, I saw my bifurcated life for what it was: a failure of daring. I had not dared to remain. More than this, I had been a show-off in my leaving. And I was still showing off—leaving there, leaving here — keeping the truth for the writing itself, hiding it away like a criminal. For what is writing, after all, but a bid for the truth? And what is truth if not the life at the very heart of failure?

HOME ON THE RANGE

I AM THE VICTIM OF A MIXED METAPHOR.
When I was twenty-one, I phoned my mother
from the other side of the world to ask whether
I should marry a man I had my doubts about.

"What doubts?" she said.

"I don't want to be stuck," I said, "and I
want to travel."

"Travel!" she shouted. "For God's sake!

When are you going to come to grips with your itchy feet?"

As phrases go, this one had power. It carried both the horror of life as a bag lady and the seduction of serious intentions—a proper education, a husband, a child, a house, and lots and lots of things to put in that house. Also, there was the issue of feet. At twenty-one, my feet were flawless. I'd even earned a bit of pocket money modeling sandals. My idea of traveling had nothing to do with tromping. Nor with youth hostels, backpacks, walking shoes that could double for a night on the town. What I wanted—what I had wanted since ever I could remember—was the vague delight of being a stranger in a strange place.

"Marry him first," my mother suggested, "and then travel."

Clearly, the home I'd grown up in was wearing thin. I'd have to come up with another. But how could I know that the man who was promising a houseboat on the Mediterranean, trips down Africa in a Land Rover, would come to embrace phrases like "discretionary income" and "fiscal irresponsibility"? Or that he would take up carpentry as a hobby, fill the house we'd bought with knotty pine and butcher block?

Every evening, every weekend, he'd descend like a woodchuck to his saws and sanders in the basement, and I, with a heap of degrees in a job market run dry, took up car pool and dinner party, factory outlet, sewing machine. Our sweet Edwardian house succumbed to bold earth tones, flokati rugs, giant pillows, Marimekko, Arabia ware, and a daily dose of *Sesame Street*.

For our first vacation, we went to a family camp in some mountains nearby. We stayed in a cabin with a tentlike roof and had our meals, kibbutz style, at long tables—some for adults, some for children. Every day, the children were organized into groups and taken away. The adults could choose their own groups. There was water polo or hiking or volleyball or pottery or macramé. I'd never been any good at Group, so I tried Sitting on Steps of Cabin with Book. This, however, had its drawbacks too. I found it hard to breathe. However much I tried, the air wouldn't go deeper than my shoulders. The camp was dusty. Dust billowed as you walked. It lodged in my clothing, up my nostrils, between my teeth.

The camp doctor looked and listened. Then he let his stethoscope drop. "It has nothing to do with the dust," he said. "You're suffering from unhappiness. I suggest you go home."

Soon after we got home, my mother phoned. "When are you coming home?" she asked. "Why do you have to live on the other side of the world?"

But I'd just got in to law school. Law school was the thing women did in the seventies. Several friends had taken it up, together with tweed suits, sensible pumps, and a multitude of high-minded causes. As a lawyer, I thought, I'd make some discretionary income of my own. I'd use it to travel indiscriminately, wherever I wanted to go.

"We'll send you a ticket," my mother said. "Come home for the Christmas holidays, when it's nice and hot."

When it came down to dates, though, my husband objected. He objected to the very idea of my going home. Home, he said, was where he was. In America. With my income as a lawyer, he pointed out, and when our child had finished college, our discretionary income would rise. And then, when we'd retired, we'd do nothing but travel. Travel here, travel there. Life would be a festival of travel.

That's when I turned down law school to become a travel agent. Three nights a week, I went to travel school. I learned how to write an airline ticket from Kalispell to Nairobi, how to work out minimum connecting times between the airports in Milan, and where to find a walking tour of Patagonia. During the day, I wrote a novel about a woman who gave up a career in medicine to take up the piano. She took a lover. And went off to Mexico with him, and then came back again to find that her husband had left her.

After working as a travel agent for a year, I sold my novel. I also began to travel in earnest. I went to ancient cities and modern ones, to rain forests and mountain ruins, to remote tropical islands and modern tourist traps. I took ocean cruises and river cruises. I stayed in hotels and palaces, in a converted convent 15,000 feet above sea level. I always traveled alone, I never traveled light, and I never had the right shoes.

Weeks before a trip, I started preparations. I cooked and froze and labeled. I drew up flow charts in several colors. I tripled my share of car pool and child swap. And then, on the way to the airport, every time, I suffered loss of breath. I wanted to turn back, to give up, to give in.

But I didn't. I went away, and I came back again. While I was home, I wrote a novel about a woman who leaves her husband and sons to go to Africa with a lover. I wrote another about a girl who grows up in Africa and leaves to live in England. Every time I came back from a trip, my house seemed smaller. It also seemed dark and cold, damp, and remote. So did my life.

"Darling!" my mother cried. "Why not settle down now and write something worthwhile? Writers can live anywhere they like, you know, all over the world."

A few weeks later, a book arrived from her, with a passage marked and starred. It was a quote by a current-day Aborigine. "A house is a good thing," said the Aborigine. "You can lock it up and go and live anywhere you please."

BY THE TIME my husband left and took his furniture, by the time the house was sold and I'd bought another one for myself, I'd got over the anxiety I'd suffered in leaving, the sadness of coming back.

What I had come to understand — sitting on verandahs where no English was spoken, riding across deserts, eating crocodile in vast colonial dining rooms — was the natural affinity between travel and fiction. Playing stranger in strange places gave me the perspective of other worlds from which to examine my own. Estrangement,

I realised, was a necessary ingredient of my work. Over the years, I began to feel more or less strange everywhere. I also felt more or less at home. Homesick for nowhere. Permanently displaced. Free to come and go at last.

THE BIG SNORE

IF YOU ARE BOTH A WRITER AND A TELLER OF
stories, people are always telling you to write
the stories that you tell. What they don't realise
is how distinct the two modes are, how different
the language for each, and how disparate the
audiences.

The tale told must adjust itself to its audience. The teller must judge timing and response,

cut as she speaks, leap, if necessary, whole seg-
ments, or flesh others out, to arrive at the denouement exactly on time. Stories told too long
lose their audiences. Stories abbreviated too
much have the sound of boredom. And boredom in the teller will kill any audience flat.

The most important distinction between the
story told and the story written, however, lies
in the fact that a storyteller controls something
that a story writer never can: who it is that actually hears the story. The storyteller can wait for
the right audience to come up. And, when it is
there, use it to effect.

If one has the audience one needs, it isn't
difficult to bring the conversation around to fit
a story one wants to tell. Couples do this all the
time, sometime as teams, with stories well re-
hearsed, or—given the public nature of an audience—for revenge on each other.

One has only to consider the subject of
snoring. Snoring stories abound. Because the
great majority of snorers seem to be men, the
stories themselves are often told by women. To

see a man—upright, shirt and tie, a wineglass held knowingly to his lips—reduced by a snoring story to a slack-jawed monster of darkness is to know the very nature of female revenge. How can he deny what he is not aware of? What she, in her treachery, may even produce witnesses to? And, if she is a good enough storyteller, she will quote details so fitting that, after a while, the audience doesn't care how faithful her account is to fact. Or who suffers in the telling.

Part of the treachery of snoring stories has to do with the fact that snoring takes place in bed and is itself so absolutely unsexy. No one wants to be known as a snorer. Nor to be laughed at on its account. And yet, snoring can be hilarious. Audiences adore a well-told snoring story. Partly because of the absurdity of snoring itself, but also because of the nature of its victims—snorer and snoree. And because its hero, snoring itself, always emerges victorious.

I told my first snoring story quite early, without any intention of revenge. I told it to illustrate a man's sweetness.

It began, in fact, the first night I ever spent with him. In a single bed. In a tiny room. No sooner had I managed, in the nine inches of bed left to me, to start sinking towards sleep, than a rumble—more like a growl, or, as I thought then, a heroic call of the wild—began to roll out of him. I had never heard anything like it. I touched him lightly with a finger. No good. I prodded a bit harder. He heaved and hauled himself over onto his side. And then there was silence. For a while. Until I was just losing consciousness, and he rolled back onto his back, and the racket started up again.

Dawn came. The sun shone into the room. He stretched an arm over for me. "Was it good for you, darling?" he murmured. "Can I bring you a cup of tea?"

"*No!*" I snapped. "And I will never spend another night in the same bed with you."

He was startled.

"You snore!" I explained.

He looked at me, mortified at the thought

that he could have betrayed so absolutely and unconsciously the man in him who had invited me into his bed in the first place.

"Come back tonight," he said. "Please! You can have the whole bed to yourself."

And so I did. And he sat in a chair, saying that he would stretch out next to me later, after I had fallen asleep. But when I woke the next morning, he was still in the chair, his head flopped forward like the victim of the executioner. He looked exhausted. He hadn't snored, but he hadn't slept either.

Still, after a night of uninterrupted sleep, I felt nothing but love for this man. Two months later we were married and buying a king-size bed. This, he assured me, would give me plenty of room to get away from the noise.

But the first night in it, and every night thereafter, the snoring returned. Torture at twenty-minute intervals.

First, I tried earplugs, every kind available. Nothing, however, was equal to the noise he made. Try tapping him gently, friends suggested. Say, "Darling, you're snoring." Turn him onto his side.

I found, however, that the very effort of saying, "Darling, you're snoring," woke me up completely. So too did heaving an adult man from his back onto his side. So too did the responses of the man himself. "No, no, I'm just going to the beach," he would say in his sleep. Or "Hang on a minute, I'll see if she's on this bus." Wide awake in the dark, I would begin to wonder what was going on in his head. I'd prod him more vigorously and demand, "Who's on the bus? What beach?" So that he, in turn, would lean over and shake my shoulder. "Wake up, darling," he'd say. "You're having a bad dream."

By now I was beginning to realise from the faces of my friends, and in the way they asked me to repeat the details, that the snoring, for all its torture, had the makings of a real story. Even the characters were right for comedy. My man happened to take himself very seriously. We had serious arguments as to whose problem it was—snorer's or snoree's. But he had also never learned to be laughed at. More than this, he was a bad sport. Suitable as the story might be, there was no way I could imagine going public with it. Not yet anyway.

Meanwhile, we continued to search for a cure. "Tennis ball in the back of pyjamas" came up one day. He had read about this somewhere and brought me a pyjama top and showed me where to sew a pocket. A tennis ball against the spine, he explained, encourages a snorer to sleep on his side.

That night in went the ball. In came my snorer, a prominent hump between his shoulders, walking seriously around to his side of the bed. Neither of us mentioned the hump. Neither of us laughed. Good night. Good night. Lights off. And then, at 3:00 A.M., there it was again—the heroic rattle, the bellow, the wheeze.

"Darling," I said, "the ball isn't working—"

"Where's the umbrella?" he shouted. "Just a minute—"

We moved on to white sound. The top of the line. Wind, sea, and rain. But they all sounded the same and provided only background to the snoring. I turned up the volume. But then the storm itself kept me awake. And woke him too. Back went the machine to the store.

I called my friends with the latest failures. At least we could laugh together, they louder than I. Without sleep my whole life seemed to be taking place three feet behind my eyes. I found myself falling asleep over my computer.

Then, one night, he came home with an announcement, "Ace bandages," he said. It was his idea, and the theory went like this: if his wrists could be tied to the side of the bed so that he couldn't roll onto his back, he wouldn't be able to snore. He was so optimistic about this idea that I, too, pretended to be full of hope. In fact, I now had my secret hope fixed on having the bedroom to myself. It was the only hope I had.

He unraveled the bandage and instructed me on how to bind his wrists in a figure eight and then to secure them to the bedpost with a reef knot. This done, I walked around to my side and climbed in. I tried not to think of what would happen if a fire broke out. Or if he needed to go to the lavatory. I fell asleep.

At 4:05, I was woken up by what sounded like a cry of pain. I sat up in alarm and switched on the light. There he was at the far side of the bed, his head twisted around and upwards like one of the Guernica horses, back arched, mouth gaping. I scrambled over him and released his hands from the bandages.

The next day, as I drooped over breakfast, the cleaning woman came to stand before me.

"Yes, Conchita?"

"Must I wash the ropes?"

"What ropes?"

"The ropes for the bed," she said, looking at the floor.

And then I understood that there was nothing for it. The story had to be told. I had tried them all out by now on this one and that one. All I needed was a denouement and the right occasion on which to tell it.

That night he took longer than usual in the bathroom. He switched off the light before coming to bed. As soon as my eyes were accustomed to the gloom, I noticed that his whole head was tightly swathed in the Ace bandage — chin to crown, round and round. Lips, cheeks, nose, and brow were squashed into the middle of his face. In the dim glow of the streetlamp I saw a large safety pin glistening over one ear.

Before dawn the next morning the bandage was off. He looked at me as soon as I woke up.

"Well?" he asked.

"It didn't work," I said. "You wheezed."

Over breakfast he asked me what people would think if we had separate bedrooms. What would it look like, marriage-wise, he wanted to know? I told him about Queen Elizabeth and her four children. I made up case histories and statistics. I reminded him that I would be just across the hall. He too. That we could cross over whenever we wished. It might be quite fun, in fact.

In fact, no sooner did people hear about our separate bedroom arrangement than women began to confide how envious they were. They catalogued the horrors of their own conjugal beds. Farting; toenail stabbing; belches and drools; blankets pulled off; blankets piled on; jumpers and yellers and weepers. I could only rejoice in my own salvation. Eight hours of uninterrupted sleep a night. The joy of silence. Good night. Good night. As simple as that.

However.

The bliss of having one's bedroom to oneself makes one reluctant to give it up. Even for a night. Even for a vacation.

We were off to France in April for a two-week conference. I suggested that we order a suite at the hotel and pay the difference. But he didn't like the idea of making an exception of himself amongst his peers. Or of having to explain the reason why.

"You don't have to explain anything," I said. "It's none of their business."

A few weeks before we were to leave, I read a small ad in a magazine. "Guaranteed Cure for Snoring," it said. There was a photograph of some sort of collar, and an address to write to, a money-back guarantee, and a price of sixty-five dollars, including batteries. I sent off the money and received the collar by return mail. That night I presented him with the gift as a gesture of reconciliation. "Let's try it out before we go," I suggested.

Carefully, he read the instructions. He inserted the batteries in the correct place, and tested the on-off switch. "It doesn't say anything about how it works," he said. He turned it on and raised it to his ear. Nothing. Then he held it to his throat as instructed and strapped it on.

"Hmm—" He clutched suddenly at his throat with both hands.

"HEL—" He fell back onto the bed, gesticulating behind his neck, beckoning me, pointing to the collar.

"Want me to help?" I asked.

He nodded furiously.

"With what?" I asked.

He pulled himself up and made some sort of fixing motion in the air with his fingers.

"Tighter?" I asked.

He shook his head and rolled his eyes.

"Looser?"

Nod, nod.

He sat up and I unsnapped the snap. As soon as it was off, he grabbed the thing from my hands. "You want to kill me!" he yelled. "It gives goddamn shocks!"

I turned away with a little cough.

"You're perverted!" he shouted. "If you think it's so goddamn funny, you wear the damned thing!"

The next day, I phoned my friends with the story. And then packaged up the collar and sent it back to the manufacturer with a letter. A letter and a cheque for sixty-five dollars came back by return mail two days before we left for Paris. The inventor was disappointed. He had never had a failure before, he said.

As soon as we got back from Paris, the subject of snoring came up suddenly, at a party, without my help. Everyone had a snoring story. Someone had snored at the symphony. Someone else had been kept awake all night by a snorer in the room next door. It was amateur stuff.

I looked at my man. He was swinging back in his chair and laughing more loudly than the stories deserved. His laughing got on my nerves. Lately the marriage itself had been getting on my nerves. On his too. We were leveling all sorts of blame at each other. Separate bedrooms ranked high for him. Snoring did for me. But there were other things too. I didn't love him anymore. He hardly ever crossed the hall. Nor did I.

And so I started the story at the beginning.

All men snore, I said, and I myself have no talent for sleeping. Nor for sharing a bed.

The audience paid attention. One woman said that she liked to have her husband next to her at night. She said his snoring comforted her. She stroked his arm. He smiled apologetically at me.

I was pleased with this. It reinforced the basis of my story—men as snorers and myself as the eccentric of the piece. I began with my first experience on the single bed. And then moved on, in one leap, to earplugs.

Everyone had something to say about earplugs. A composer explained that they are not designed to eliminate highs and lows. The subject began to veer off into subway trains and ghetto blasters.

Quickly I brought it back with a rendition of the trumpeting snore I knew so well. They laughed. A few people looked from me to him. I moved on to the tennis ball and loped around the table as Quasimodo. They bellowed. Then I bound up my chin with a table napkin. I held my wrists together for a rendition of Guernica. By the time I got to the maid and the ropes, they were mine. They had forgotten him in the audience, and so had I.

As soon as the laughing died down, I began on separate bedrooms and crossing the hall. For the sake of the story, I moved the guaranteed cure to Paris. But, no sooner had I started on inserting the batteries into the collar than he stood up.

"That's a lie!" he said.

"Oh, go on!" said someone, "We want to hear."

But he stood where he was, glowering at me.

I knew I had to work quickly. I clutched my hands to my throat. I shot both legs forward.

They shrieked. They fell onto the table. They wiped their eyes.

"Rubbish!" he shouted.

"Give her a chance!" someone said.

"The next morning at breakfast—"

He pushed back his chair and slammed out of the room.

They watched him go and then turned back to me. "Go on, go on," they said. "What happened?"

Suddenly I hesitated. I knew that the ending I had been working towards didn't fit the story. Or even the audience. But they were all looking at me. They were waiting.

"Oh, I don't know," I said, "I don't know what they thought had been going on up there."

They laughed politely, but it wasn't the same.

"Great story," someone said.

People began to stand. One of them tapped me on the shoulder as she passed. "You should write that," she said.

I nodded, wondering whether he had left with the car and how I would get home.

Someone announced the time.

I thought of what I would say to him now. And where we would go from here.

DOING TIME

IT TOOK MY FIRST TEACHING JOB FOR ME
to understand what I really wanted to do with
my life. I was just out of graduate school and
considered lucky to have been hired even temporarily by a large university. And yet, from the
minute I first entered the classroom I was gripped
by an old and very familiar panic, something that

had visited me since early childhood whenever I felt myself stuck in a situation in which I didn't feel at home. I suffered what I can only describe as a loss of self, a loss which seemed to preclude all hope for the future, all freedom, all joy.

Looking back on that time now, I see that the malaise had little to do with the nature of the actual task at hand: introducing a class of undergraduates, composed largely of Vietnam veterans, to Shakespeare, Jane Austen, and a selection of English lyric poetry. Had the class been filled with classically educated literary enthusiasts, it would, I feel sure, have produced the same result, if a little more slowly. It was the classroom itself that seemed to bring with it the threat of a life circumscribed by such classrooms—such desks, such office hours, such falafel vendors and poster shops and tenure committees and memos from the Chair.

One day, walking out of the ugly building in which I taught and into the California sunshine, I stopped for a moment to look around at the students massing, the Hare Krishnas dancing, a drab woman professor making her way back to the English department. I was twenty-eight years old, married, with a small child, and still I was asking myself the question I had been asking for as long as I could remember: Is this what you want? Is this what you really want?

Many times over the years, and in any number of different circumstances, I had asked myself just such a question. But only now did an answer arrive without a hint of prevarication: *No.* This was *not* what I wanted, not now, not ever. Moreover, I knew in that moment exactly what I *did* want—what I had wanted, in fact, since ever I had dreamed of a future for myself, had I only been able to give it the legitimacy of words. I wanted to write and I wanted to travel.

SIXTEEN YEARS LATER—with marriage, two novels, a world of travel and a career as a part-time travel agent behind me—I was back in the classroom. The invitation had come from a large university in the Southwest, offering a decent sum to spend two semesters teaching creative writing. This time, there hadn't even been a question of what I really wanted: I needed money. The modest advance on my last book was long since gone, the next book was hardly on the page, and working full-time as a travel agent would have paid little more than the cost of my travel, leaving no time at all to write.

So I packed up my car and drove across the country to a city lost in the fold of the Rand McNally map. And then suddenly, after fifteen years, it was back to dips and chips on a Saturday night and Marvin Gaye with the rug rolled up. Not to mention "lay" for "lie," split infinitives, falafel stands, office hours, memos from the Chair—the whole baggage, in short, of my new and unnervingly familiar patron, the Academy.

Had marriage been this bad? I tried to remember.

"Ma'am," said a C student, "I just want you to know I'm shootin' for an A." He was a young man who seemed to suffer incurably, like so many of the others, from television ear ("Son,

I'm leaving." "But, Dad, just think of Mom, think of what this will do to her." "I am thinking of your mother, son. Trust me. One day you will be old enough to understand all this.") He was taking my Undergraduate Creative Writing: Fiction class "to better sharpen his verbal skills," he claimed. The fact was, he said, he was headed for law school. He needed the hours and he needed the grades.

I stared at him, wondering what my writing life would have been like had I become a lawyer. Lawyers could work part-time. As it was, my writing itself had come to a standstill. Every time I switched on the computer, I remembered the student stories I had to grade. And then, once they were read, it was as if all the vigour had dropped out of my own desire to write. Writing felt like homework I was setting for myself in a subject of which I had long since grown tired.

Every day, letters arrived from my mother. "What are you writing?" she wanted to know. "Don't put your all into teaching, darling, or you'll regret it." She understood quite well what she was saying. Given greater talent than she had, she would have stayed on the English stage. As it was, she put much of her own all into her acting school, kicking off her shoes and hiking up her skirt to demonstrate, yet again, to a hopeless student how to fall down a flight of stairs without killing herself.

In the office next to mine was a famous Indian writer, also visiting for the year. Recently he had become a bestseller in India when one of his novels was turned into a television series. His office was filled with women in saris all talking at once — this one was a daughter, that one a daughter-in-law. They lived in a furnished apartment nearby and all came to the university together, carrying marvelous-smelling food.

"What are you doing about grading??" I shouted at him. He was very old and quite deaf, and hardly seemed to understand why he was there at all. But I was in transports of exasperation myself, subject to the assaults and imprecations of students every time I handed back a set of graded stories. With every week that passed, I felt stupider, less sure of my right to be teaching at all, let alone grading. Perhaps, after all, the student writing of his father's "uncircumsided" penis was not to be faulted for his English if, as the story seemed to imply, he had suffered the repeated assaults of such a weapon as a boy himself. But then again, so what? Why did such a thing have to land up in *my* Undergraduate Creative Writing: Fiction class when it belonged more properly with social services?

"How do you teach them writing?" I shouted at the Indian writer. "How do you teach them to write?"

"Oh! Teaching!" he laughed. "Either they are reading my books, or they are not!"

I made my way back to the Versailles townhouse complex in the spirit of an outcast. It was ninety-eight degrees. My car had no air-conditioning, and my townhouse itself was infested with crickets. So was the one across the pool. My friend the handyman had told me that the redhead who lived there was a medical student and had two diaphragms under her bed, one on each side, both of which he had sprayed for crickets.

Gazing across the pool, with its dozens of crickets skittering on the surface, I wondered if things would have been easier had I become a doctor. Doctors could work part-time. The redhead herself was home a lot, and men came and went there constantly. One wore an army uniform and carried a ghetto blaster. Another wore Bermuda shorts and a baseball cap turned around backwards. When I had instructed the students in my class to remove their baseball caps, they had complained to the chairman. He called me in and asked whether I would please relent. Things are different in this country, he explained to me. Students tend to wear hats the way they wear shoes. In addition, they have concerns about "hat hair." Perhaps I should consider the teaching evaluations they would be turning in at the end of the semester. Such things counted for future employment, he said.

It was at about this point that it began to dawn on me that I had landed myself in a situation in which the inmates were running the institution. I might have known. I had arrived at graduate school in New York in the late sixties, right at the onset of the Age of Relevance — a time when, as Isaiah Berlin lamented, a whole generation of youth confused crudity with sincerity.

What I was encountering now was simply the logical result of that revolution — the supreme relevance of the self in an institution that had come to depend for its continuance on the pleasing of that self. It was a self that took its reference not from history, philosophy, and literature, but from psychology, a variety conveniently adjusted to the pursuit of personal happiness. And so the Age of Relevance had become the Age of the Self.

It is one thing to understand the points of the compass, quite another to use them in order to find one's way in a life circumscribed by one's own refusals — the refusal, in my case, to consider permanent full-time employment and the refusal to abandon the freedom to travel.

Once the year in the Southwest was over and I was back in California, I found myself again facing the problem of how I was going to earn a living. Freelance writing was all very well, but it was haphazard, unsuited to a temperament prone to anxiety. And so, when other offers of temporary teaching positions started coming in, I would accept them.

And then off I would go again—over the Rockies, up to the Pacific Northwest—to live for a few months in yet another sadly furnished apartment, in yet another grim university town. Even though I never accepted more than one teaching stint per year, I found that the teaching itself was beginning to order my life. When I was free of it, I stayed home and wrote like mad—fiction, essays, articles for magazines, many of them involving travel. But then, sooner or later, it would be time to pack up again, to go off again to do my time somewhere else.

After a while, I joined the faculty in a low-residency MFA program on the East Coast. It didn't pay much, but, except for the ten-day residency itself, it allowed me to stay home, teaching by correspondence. And when I did have to fly off again for the next residency, it was to go into the company of friends.

Low-residency writing programs and summer conferences provide a sort of peripatetic café society for writers, supplying what nothing else can, certainly not a university department: the chance to make friends with writers from all over the country, all of us doing time together for a week or two, and then going back to our disparate lives. Most of the writers in such programs have other jobs—teaching or editing. Some don't need the money at all; they go for each other's company, for the audience of students, for the swapping of gossip, the give-and-take of sympathy about the travails of the classroom itself.

And so when, after some years, I was offered a permanent half-time professorship at a large university within easy reach of home, I took it with a backward glance at what I was leaving behind. Certainly, there was no question of turning the offer down: the job came with tenure, full benefits, and a proper salary to live on. Café society or no, I was tired of struggling, and longed for what I could only think of as peace. It had been ten years since I had taken that first creative writing job in the Southwest, and I was tired of moving, tired, too, of worrying about where the next job would come from, and where it would take me to.

On Open House Day in the new job, I lined up as instructed along one wall of a bare classroom, with several other members of the Creative Writing division. We were there to be interviewed by the potential consumers of our wares. With writing programs thick on the ground, colleges and universities compete fiercely for students. "Let's play up the climate," one of the teachers suggested as the students began to file in. "Someone point out that we can ride bikes here for most of the year."

We. Our. Suddenly I felt as if I had married

the wrong man again. Working as a peripatetic teacher, even in a low-residency program, I had managed to maintain a rather outspoken position on the teaching of writing that did not, somehow, seem to be at odds with the terms of my employment. Now, however, I found myself stiffening with pride and embarrassment as my turn came to sell myself to the customers. I heard my voice — tight, clipped, resentful — and longed to bolt into the air before things got even worse. But question time had come around and hands were going up. What is your workshop philosophy? someone wanted to know. Which writers do you most admire? What do you consider the benefits of an MFA degree? What have you published? What percentage of your students make it as writers?

THE ONLY STUDENTS I have ever taught who were more ambitious than MFA students were domestic servants in South Africa. I taught them Afrikaans at a night school run by students at the university I attended. It was a hated language, but one they needed if they were to achieve a school-leaving certificate and, with it, the hope of a better life.

And now here was that desperate hope again, the hope brought this time to bear on making it as a writer in a culture mired in the worship of celebrity. Considering the odds for success as a member of a garage band or as an actor in an audition lineup, those for the writing student in an MFA program are not bad. All around us, after all, are the successes that have been generated by such programs. And if the books themselves often seem a little too clever, a little heavy on craft and light on substance — if books five hundred pages long, discussing subtle but allegedly profound shifts within a relationship seem to be "in," as a judge for a major fiction award recently complained — well, who, after all, has not experienced subtle and profound shifts? Who has not grown up? At least to the age of nineteen or twenty? Who, in a nation of immigrants, cannot go back a generation or two and find something that might pass for exotic? Ethnically engaging? Heartrendingly pitiful? Or even sublimely ordinary?

Apart from regular MFA candidates, there are legions of other writing students, particularly in the summer workshops, casual workshops, the low-residency MFA programs—people who have lives already established and are looking, in their workshops, for a teacher, a sponsor, or, at the very least, for the company of others who write. Doctors, personal trainers, screenwriters, professional gamblers, corporate lawyers, teachers, housewives, landscape gardeners, librarians, cod fishermen, TV executives—I have taught them all. And if there is not a wealth of talent among them, still, it is here that one is more likely to find a kindred spirit and some real readers.

The average MFA student may read more than the average undergraduate student of literature—the sort of undergraduate who, in an essay on Primo Levi's *Survival in Auschwitz,* can include a sentence that begins, "When Primo and the other campers came in from the fields at night"—but still a whole generation of would-be writers in the academy seems to have only the most cursory acquaintance with the literary canon. The contemporary fiction-writing student is more likely to be familiar with contemporary fiction, particularly that which has emerged from writing programs like his own.

It is here that I am most at sea. My reading of contemporary fiction is spotty at best, based largely on the recommendations of others. When I am asked which writers I most admire, I panic, I go blank. If I am lucky, I remember a few names, and, even then, the writers are likely either to be dead or about to be. All I can think of are the writers I haven't been able to stand—books I have hurled across the room, one of which took the corner off my dressing-table mirror.

Falling back on the greats is easier, far easier. I might start off a workshop with a bit of Proust, for instance:

> The beautiful things we shall write if we have the talent are inside us, indistinct,

like the memory of melody which delights us though we are unable to recapture its outline. Those who are obsessed by this blurred memory of truth they have never known are the men who are gifted. . . . Talent is like a sort of memory which will enable them finally to bring this indistinct music closer to them, to hear it clearly, to note it down.

A writer, I say, must not only have a story to tell, but a story that he *must* tell. And, in order to do so, he must struggle to find a voice. Whether he works with or against the natural iambic metre of the English language, the writer must be in love with language, with the words themselves, the *sound* of the words on the page, the music they make in meaning. He must love them not so much in order to *express* the self as to discover *a* self, and, through it, his province, his territory, the territory of his story.

What do you mean by "voice"? they ask.

Trying to explain something I understand

only sketchily myself, I resort to metaphors—a thumbprint on the page, the inimitable sound of Callas. I pull out some opening paragraphs—Duras, Naipaul, Graham Greene, William Trevor. Listen to the music of the words, I say, the rhythms, the gorgeous way the rhythms and the meanings converge. They nod, they do see the point, they make notes. Most are already teaching writing themselves, to undergraduates. Most of them already think of themselves as writers and teachers.

I move on to a discussion of their manuscripts, reminding them that we are not in a therapy session, that the fact that they may like or dislike, approve or disapprove, of a character is not relevant to the literary merits or shortcomings of the piece at hand. The story I begin with is full of shortcomings, but it also delivers a line that has already made it into the burgeoning pool of such offerings among my writer friends—a pool that goes a small way towards redeeming the whole enterprise itself.

I read the line aloud: "'Give it to me in the

ass,' Mom said. I could hear from her voice that she didn't mean it."

The students look up nervously. They consider me a bit Jean Brodie-ish, not to be counted on as a pal.

"One could put this into internal monologue," I suggest. "That might help to flesh out the character of the narrator." I read the line again. But as soon as I get to "ass," the class falls into an uproar of delight and the writer himself, a dear boy trying to seem dangerous, pulls his knitted cap down over his ears and forehead.

Questions? I say, to calm them down. How do you build a character with internal monologue? someone asks. How do you set up an unreliable narrator? How do you shape the narrative arc?

I shake my head. Despite all my years in creative writing classrooms, I still have no idea how to pretend to unravel the mystery. These concerns are red herrings, I say. So are the relative merits of the first, second, or third persons, active and passive voice. I tell them about W. C. Fields—how I heard that after reading an analysis of his juggling, he couldn't juggle for six years. They laugh; they know the feeling, they say.

And I feel like a fraud. Week after week in come their stories—some just committed to the page, some rewritten so many times and under the aegis of so many different workshops that the writer himself has lost all sense of the authenticity of the piece if ever it was to be found there in the first place. What can I do about this? How can I help someone breathe life into a flat and pointless piece of writing? I cannot. If there are teachers who know how to work from the abstract to the concrete, I am not one of them.

So what can I do in a world in which bad stories may well be written by likable people? I can forget the writers. I *do* forget them as I sit reading paragraph after paragraph of more or less mediocre writing, my blood rising yet again at the presumption of an audience, *any* audience for this, let alone the serious attention of an irascible writer with one foot nailed to the ground for the duration of the semester.

And then, one day, in comes a story with an opening paragraph so good that it fills me with a rush of hope — hope not so much for the writer as for myself. Reading on, page after page, I feel the weight of the sham lifting from me — the awful burden of having to take seriously a piece of writing that should be consigned to the bin.

The story is, in fact, the second draft that I have seen, and it has been completely transformed. The student himself has not followed any of my suggestions; he's done better, much better. I find myself envying him his furious youth, his selfish, single-minded determination. Even though he is among the legions of students who are socially and conversationally tone-deaf — handing over his manuscript with, "Here is the story you need to read," a phrase that brings on instant rage and usually guarantees scant attention for the work — I cannot now help scrawling, "Wonderful! Brilliant rewrite!"

The happiest teachers are, perhaps, those who are most comfortable in the role of parent or of mentor. I am not. I might advise a good student to get himself out of the academy as quickly as he can, but I have no stake in his future beyond wishing him well. When yet another person says, "But surely it is gratifying to come across talent?" I have to say that it is more of a relief than a gratification.

I am not a natural liar. I find it almost impossible to pretend to admire a poor piece of writing, either in manuscript or in print, even if it is written by someone I like. Being asked to deliver a quote for the jacket of a bad book casts me into acute misery. I suspect that this difficulty, like so much else in my writing life, goes back again to my mother, to the unquestioning standard to which she held all art, the real despair she suffered when, having set up an acting school rather late in life, she found herself faced with the task of teaching acting to the untalented. Confucius was said to have turned his back on the untalented. Had my mother been entitled to do so, I feel sure she would have pushed them off a cliff.

When, as an adult, I found in a Japanese piano teacher a woman of fierce and uncompromising standards, I felt immediately at home. Despite her almost incomprehensible English, she led me further towards an understanding of the art of the piano than all my years of lessons as a child had done.

As a piano student, I was not much different from any number of the writing students I was to encounter when I myself began to teach — an enthusiastic amateur. If there was a difference between them and me, it lay, perhaps, in the fact that I did not for a moment consider myself a pianist. Such a thing would have been both ludicrous and presumptuous in someone of minimal talent and inadequate application. I was taking the lessons because I loved to play, because I wanted to play better, and because a weekly lesson with a master of the instrument forced me not only to practise regularly, but also to do so in a way that would make her less likely to push me off a cliff.

To my surprise, when my own child turned seven and I asked the teacher please to take her on, she refused. "I never teaching a Caucasian children, never a Japanese neither. Too middle class, too looking around. I teach a Chinese. Chinese understand excellence."

I was delighted with this. And so, after a decent interval, I brought up the subject again. And then again. When, at last, she relented, she did so with a few provisos: I must stop taking lessons myself ("Never teach a mother and a daughter same time"), the girl had to practice for a certain number of hours a day, and I should buy a grand piano for her to practice on. The old upright I'd had for years would only encourage bad habits, she said.

And so began my daughter's seven years with the only teacher she was ever to encounter who maintained a standard of perfection unadulterated by false encouragement. Within a few years, she was playing far beyond my own abilities. She was also, on the teacher's insistence, enrolled at the Conservatory, taking lessons in solfège and the history of music. It was only when as a teenager she rebelled and refused to go on that I came to understand that, although she had a nice touch and a passable technique, she lacked what is essential in any art: a vocation.

As it turned out, that first creative writing class in the Southwest had let me in easily: the students there did not envision themselves as writers. Most of them were only taking the course as a way to fulfill an English requirement. Subsequent university positions, however, took me right into the teeth of a culture of professional writing students, a culture that had given rise to what was fast becoming the cash cow of many humanities departments—graduate programs in creative writing.

A creative writing program relies for its status on the relative fame of its faculty and on the publishing successes of its students. The publishing industry itself is quite alert to these possibilities: writing schools produce books that will be taught in writing schools at worst; at best, and with a bit of luck, some of these books break through into general readership. Generations of books have by now emerged from such programs, and the process has turned a number of unknown writing students and ex–writing students into household names, either liberating them, at least temporarily, from having to teach in a writing program themselves or guaranteeing them a job in such a program.

That talent itself might have little to do with such success is neither here nor there. Talent is the naked emperor of writing programs. How, for instance, does one approach the subject in a workshop that may well be devoid of even one student showing a hint of it? Mentioning talent serves only to make everyone nervous. (Do I have it? Does she? Anyway, who is she to judge? I just got a personal rejection from the *New Yorker.*) Mentioning vocation, on the other hand, is likely to make everyone feel comfortable. In a world that confuses the calling to write with the desire to be a writer, "vocation" is just another word for ambition.

When someone has a story accepted for publication or a book proposal engages the interest of a big editor, it is as if an electric current of hope and envy has been run through the group. How can one quarrel with this? Or with the considerable advance that yet another student might be offered for a novel one finds unreadable oneself? How can one tell student writers, most of whom place their trust in the efficacy of group learning, that unless they can turn themselves into solitaries, driven to ride single-mindedly over all obstacles, all reverses, all failures and discouragements, taking what they need ruthlessly, discarding the rest—unless they can become what it is, in fact, impossible to become because one must be born that way, talented or not—there is little to be gained by taking a writing workshop beyond a few years free to write, the blessing of imposed deadlines, and the company of other student writers?

One cannot. Or, at least, *I* cannot, not beyond telling them at the outset, even though they will not believe me (Why should they? Why, after all, have I taken such a job?) that, to my mind, writing cannot be taught. That workshops can be dangerous. That the best I can do as a teacher is to function as a good editor, to help a student train his ear so that he can come to edit himself. That unless the student plans to spend his life moving from workshop to workshop, he will need to be able to rely on his own ear. And that if he does move from workshop to workshop, he is doomed to lose his sense of hearing anyway.

"But it's hard to hear ourselves," they say, "when all we hear is your voice—Start here! Sink this! Where's the story?"

I understand. I am in the same boat myself. With the classroom so present in my life, everything I write begins to sound like a teacher writing—intended, crafted, lifeless, and too clever by half. Teaching writing has returned me to the sort of cleverness I needed as a student of literature — searching for meanings, tying up loose ends. "There are many forms of stupidity," said Thomas Mann, "and cleverness is the worst."

When I open a book or even a magazine, I find myself scouring it for things to point out in the classroom — a transition well achieved, a change in point of view, a turning point, a leap into the future on nothing more than a brush-stroke. Try this voice for yourselves, I might suggest. Copy it. See how she begins, right into the middle of the story? No groundwork? No explanation? Why not try that?

And yet, even as I say this, I know that, except for the very few, trying on another writer's voice will carry them only so far towards finding one of their own. For the real part of the journey, injunctions are useless. Lost myself in the language of injunction, lost for the real work of a writer — listening, writing, listening — my ability to disappear when I sit at my desk, to sink into that other world, beyond thought, beyond analysis, is gone. I have become both too clever and too stupid to write. What I am suffering — this

cleverness, this stupidity—is the creative equivalent of an autoimmune disease. And it is ongoing. It lasts right up until the day I can emerge
from the classroom and step out into the future
again. And sometimes for longer than that.

Meanwhile, in come the students during office hours, one after the other, and there I am,
longing, despite myself, to be able to give them
something to hope for. I wish I could tell the
young woman sinking into the chair on the
other side of my desk that she should turn her
back on all this, return to her life as a physiother-
apist, write as a hobby if she has to. What she is
really after, it seems to me, is glamour. If I told
her that the life of a writer is not glamorous, she
would laugh. Without its terrors, it may well
seem glamorous to her. But she knows nothing
of such terror. She doesn't even have a clue that
the story she is clutching in her lap is beyond
anyone's help, that it has no voice, no characters,
no story. She has paid a lot to be in this program
and I am paid to help her through it.

And I like her. She is personable, funny, polite, respectful. She doesn't send me e-mails that open with "Hi there, pal!" She does not tell me how excited she is by her own writing, how gratified. Nor is she creeping or bumptious. I have long since learned that modesty and good manners are not to be expected in the academy, a world in which students eat in class, answer their cell phones, leave the classroom without excusing themselves. This young woman commits none of these offenses. Nor does she ask me, as other graduate students have, for suggestions of "fictional novels" to read. She is not uneducated. And yet, sitting in my study chair at home the night before, her story on my lap, I forgot completely the pleasant young woman behind the awful story she had written. "Where's the story?" my pencil raged in the margin. "Who cares?" "Make me care!"

"But how do I make you care?" she asks now, taking a chocolate from the bowl I keep for just such occasions. I would rather talk with this young woman about anything other than her story—the environmentally friendly car she's just bought, the amusing mother on whom much of the story is based. But she doesn't want from me what she can have from her friends. She wants to talk, writer to writer. She wants answers. And she wants progress.

Progress. There is hardly a student who doesn't believe in it as a right of registration in the program, who doesn't assume that it goes hand-in-hand with encouragement. But how could I encourage this student when there isn't even a paragraph on which to hang an edit, not even a line? If there were, the result could be salutary, at least for the purposes of the workshop. I could have her looking up in delight at the sound of her own prose moving the story across the page, the others too. Other than palavering on about the so-called writing process — quoting others, playing myself for the audience of the workshop — editing to effect is the only true delight that I know how to deliver, all I can teach that I consider worth having.

She flaps through the pages on her lap. "I mean, like, half the workshop thinks I should put the epiphany at the end," she says, "and the other half doesn't. What do you think? Would it help if I factored in some dialogue?"

I say that if I showed my work before it was sturdy enough to receive criticism, I would be as confused as she is, that this confusion is a hazard built into the very idea of a workshop. I quote Donald Hall: the problem with workshops, he said, is that they trivialize art by minimizing the terror.

She laughs. Stupidity is not her problem; lack of talent is.

As it happens, she has caught me on a particularly bad day. I have just realised that the novel on which I have been laboring for eighteen months — the novel to which I was counting on returning when the semester was over — is hopeless, every sentence in it a lie. Who am I then to fall into despair over having to take their bad prose seriously when I am in such despair over my own? Who do I think I am? Balzac?

"But I can't think of any other way to tell the reader what they must know," she says.

"What *he* must know!" I say. "And *never,* never try to *tell* the reader anything!"

She looks up, alarmed.

"And *never, never* use dialogue to deliver in-formation!" I hear my voice rising. If I could, I would tell her what is really troubling me — that I am being paid back for the sham I am taking part in week after week, month after month, that trying to explain what is essentially a mystery, I have shut the door on that mystery for myself. But she would only laugh again. To her, I am a successful writer with a job that leaves me time to write. I write, I travel, I teach. It is all she thinks she wants for herself.

"Dialogue," I say more gently, "is the poetry in the prose. It gives air to the narrative." These are well-worn phrases, phrases I have used over many years of teaching. In fact, they have lost their meaning for me, if ever they had any to start off with.

"Air?"

"Pacing, timing, rhythm."

"What about characterisation? Doesn't that

demote characterisation to a sort of subset of colour?"

I give up. I might be settled into classroom life more easily now than I was before — my style defined, my injunctions at the ready— but I am at home in the way a foreign student, doomed to spend a season in a strange country, comes to feel at home. I have become a cartoon of myself for an audience of strangers.

And yet, after every workshop the evaluations come in, and, to my continuing surprise, most are laudatory. I am praised for being encouraging. *Encouraging?* "Caring and sensitive," they say, "constructive," "inspirational." Are they mad? I might be pleased by the praise, but I am quite concerned that the job is turning me into a dancing ape. On the other hand, the ones who quarrel with my "harshness," my "negativity" have me angry and resentful. And so I am caught in the teacher's trap — the trap of wanting to be liked.

Performance can be a heady thing, especially with an audience of acolytes. Over the years, I have polished my classroom act into one that seems to work well, at least for the more resilient among the students, the ones who, like myself, feel swindled by false encouragement. Even so, they persist in being encouraged. And I, straddling the chasm between half truths and half lies, search for something to say that will leave us all morally intact. ("Do you think we're going straight to hell for this?" a fellow writing teacher asks, peering around my door. "Do you?")

Hell, in fact, is never very far away. Writing itself is a performance, a sort of magic act, played out in the dark, in silence. Trying to find one's way back to it after the public noise of teaching can take weeks or even months. Several times, between teaching stints, I have not been able to find my way back at all, so that when I do return to the classroom, I am angry and full of blame. And yet whose fault is it if I have made this bargain in the first place? My parents', for not having had the wherewithal to leave me a trust fund? My husband's, for departing an unendurable marriage? My own, for not having had the courage to trust my writing to see me through?

"Write without pay until someone offers pay," Mark Twain suggested. "If nobody offers pay within three years, the candidate may look upon this circumstance as a sign . . . that sawing wood is what he was intended for."

Before the burgeoning of creative writing departments, writers who could not make ends meet by their books, or by writing reviews or for newspapers or for Hollywood, or by editing journals, or by marrying money, or by working in a profession of one sort or another—those writers would indeed drop out of the market. Not so now. Now most writers without independent means seem either to be looking for teaching jobs or complaining about the ones they do have. And one can only wonder how one would have fared oneself without one? Sawing wood? Sewing on buttons in the dry cleaner?

And yet, earlier forms of patronage make the academy seem mild by comparison. And also, paradoxically, more dangerous. Consider Machi-avelli, for instance, out of favour with the de' Medicis, furiously writing *The Prince* to get him-self back in. Would he have been moved to write this masterpiece from within the cosy circle of patronage? More than this, would he have sur-vived as a writer had he not, in fact, achieved his aim and had himself readmitted?

There are writers who are brought down by teaching, all the life gone out of their work, And there are writers who take up the work of edit-ing other people's manuscripts, few of which are destined to make it into the light. To have to pretend to take seriously the job of improving an unworthy piece of writing because one is being paid by the writer to do so is, perhaps, the most dangerous compromise of all.

IT HAS ALWAYS taken me a while to adjust to a new rhythm of life, particularly when that rhythm is not one of my own making. Still, over the years, I have come to understand that the freedom I enjoyed as a wife-and-mother who wrote and traveled was not much different from what I now have as a professor with half the year off to write — an illusion. And that what I still seem to be longing for, almost thirty years after I walked out of that first classroom of Vietnam veterans, is what I thought I had discovered then, in those few moments, standing in the California sun — a shape for the future that brings with it hope.

But how much more future can one want for oneself? And how long can one go on wanting it? Most of my future I have already spent. Here I am at the beginning of what is left of it, in a splendid eighteenth-century château that looks out over lawns, roses, vineyards, fields of baled hay, and Lake Geneva in the distance. I have been invited here to work for a few weeks in the company of other writers, lifted out of my life and given back to myself. I unpack my clothes, go to the casement window to look out at the mountains across the lake. I am only at the start of my half year free of the classroom, and already the weight of its claim has lifted. It began to lighten when the wheels of the plane left the ground and was gone with the first sip of wine.

I sit down at the beautiful desk of inlaid wood and read through my file of notes. I have set aside my novel and come here to write an essay. For the past months of teaching, I have been wondering how I would get down to the truth of the subject, where I should begin.

"When I left teaching to become a travel agent," I write, "I was just out of graduate school, married, with a child, and suffering acutely from a madness to be free. Being locked into any situation has always worked on me in this way. And yet, with this job, I wasn't even locked in. I was simply filling in for a professor who was suffering from a nervous breakdown ..."

TAMING THE GORGON

A MOTHER CAN BE AS TROUBLESOME IN A story as she is in life. There she stands, barrier or conduit, between her daughter and the future — between the girl and the world in which she must make her way. Whatever the girl does must be done either with the help of or in spite of her mother, something that can complicate a story in ways that the writer might not wish.

And so, to eliminate the trouble, writers down through the ages have killed mothers off, particularly mothers of girls, and usually before the action even begins. Childbirth is a favourite means—this way a girl has no chance of remembering anything about her mother beyond what she has been told. Out into the world she must go, fresh off the half shell, as open to danger and desire as her creator chooses her to be.

Consider simply the daughters in Shakespeare. Consider Desdemona, Isabella, Miranda, Viola, Kate, Ophelia, Jessica, Goneril, Regan, and Cordelia—where are their mothers? Where is Emma Woodhouse's mother? Jane Eyre's? Catherine Earnshaw's? Emma Bovary's? Dorothea Brooke's? Becky Sharp's? Glencora Palliser's? Isabel Archer's? Certainly, there are surrogates abounding—aunts and stepmothers, plenty of those. But aunts and stepmothers, troublesome as they may be, are without the complex biological and psychological claim of a mother.

This is not to say that there are no mothers of girls to be found in literature. Of course there are. *Pride and Prejudice, Mill on the Floss, To the Lighthouse, The Lover, Lolita*—these are a few that come to mind. It is just that, throughout literature, and until the recent rash of mother-centred fiction and memoir—engendered, one presumes, because social politics have brought mothers into the light over the last three or four decades—until recently, mothers of girls have usually been either sentimentalized minor figures, or absent altogether.

And yet where would *Pride and Prejudice* be without Mrs. Bennet to complicate the action? Without Mr. Darcy's misgivings about a marriage with the daughter of such a woman? And without the moral complexity of Elizabeth Bennet's growing acknowledgement of the justice of such an objection? Where would *To the Lighthouse* be without Mrs. Ramsay?

"My mother, my love," wrote Marguerite Duras, "we're ashamed of her, I'm ashamed of her in the street outside the school, when she drives up to the school in her old Citroën B12 everyone looks, but she, she doesn't notice anything, ever, she ought to be locked up, beaten, killed. She looks at me and says, Perhaps you'll escape. Day and night, this obsession. It's not that you have to achieve anything, it's that you have to get away from where you are."

The Lover, in a sense, rests on this obsession.

Once, when I complained to a friend — a littérateur of some order — that I was writing something that didn't seem to have any heart in it, he said, "Ask yourself what obsesses you and write about that."

It was a useful question. Obsessions tend to be so familiar and so intimate as to occur not as ideas but as images, as daydreams barely acknowledged in the noise of daily life. My own, the ones that had accompanied me throughout youth and onward, tended towards a dream of leaving home, and also a vision of returning, both somehow cloaked in an aura of magnificence. Over the years, I had written quite a bit around such obsessions, and yet only when I read that passage of Duras's did I trace their origin to my own mother.

My mother was an actress. Before I was born, she was also a singer of some local note. She was a woman of little beauty and great style. She was also proud and fierce, and she married a man, my father, who was not only her superior socially in the small society in which they both grew up, but also younger, very beautiful, charming, and well educated. He loathed work, loved cricket, rowing, golf, and being adored by women, which came to include his own daughters. My mother, by contrast, was edgy and serious, with her mind eternally on the great world beyond and the work that was to be done in it. Had she not perforce been the wife, she would certainly have been the husband.

Unlike my father, what she wanted was to have consequence in the world, a consequence nicely balanced by a husband and a home to go back to, the sort of life with "something-more-to-it-than-wife-and-mother, darling" that she was always wishing on her own daughters. She was also childish, volatile, jealous, and prone to towering rages and mighty sulks. No end of trouble, indeed.

Right up until her death at ninety-four or ninety-seven (she lied; it was impossible to get to the bottom of it), I spent a great deal of time trying to work out when or if ever she was off-stage. The answer, I think, is, never. Not even after sinking into craziness, not even in her very old age — supine and catatonic and blind. She may not have known that she was playing "dying old woman," but that is how she seemed to me — a woman at the end of her life playing the part of a small, pale, ancient, helpless bird. And playing it rather poorly.

Once, as a girl, I asked her why she had returned to South Africa after her years at the Royal Academy of Dramatic Art and the Royal College of Music in London. Without hesitation, she said, "Because I didn't have the talent to make it to the top there." At other times, when I asked again, she said, "I didn't have the looks" or "I would have spent my whole career in character parts—the maid carrying in the tea tray and so forth." And once she said, "I wanted to be a big fish in a small bowl." I don't think she took pride in this sort of candour. What I do know is that she was too proud to lie about what mattered to her most—the theatre, and, beyond that, the whole world of the arts.

I could never stand the theatre myself. Year in, year out, it was torment to have to sit through rehearsals, and then through opening night. It did not occur to me that I could refuse to go, any more than it would occur to the child of a conductor to flee the sound of music. Nor did I even understand how much I hated it—or even *that* I hated it. Going to the theatre was simply a fact of life, like going to school (which I hated too).

And then, at the age of twenty-two, on my first trip to London, I went to a production of

Feydeau's *A Flea in Her Ear*. There, on stage, were Olivier, Gielgud, and Richardson all at once, and all, apparently, having a marvelous time. There was no straining, no prating, no gesturing, no projecting to the last row of the stalls. One minute into the play, they achieved for me what, until that moment, I had only experienced in film—the complete dissolution of the barrier between performer and audience. As I watched, I forgot entirely where I was and why. I managed to forget myself.

Looking back on that performance now, I think that it was when Gielgud began taking his perfect time removing a pair of gloves—the audience in an uproar of delight—that, without even knowing it, I began to shift my mother into a broader context, one in which she glimmered considerably less brightly. The context itself was magnificent indeed, its confines extending so far beyond the world we shared that I could never, after that, see myself in quite the same way either. Perhaps this is the point to which all pleasure in art tends—the expansion of human understanding, of ways of feeling, ways of seeing.

And there was something more. Behind the shape and form given to the complexities of love in Feydeau's farce — a minuet of action, reaction, and resolution — behind it lay the mystery of life itself. The order of the play was the order of art, its resolution as far from a solution to life's mystery as art is from the industry of psycho-salvation.

We are living in a culture that seems to believe that by unloading blame — on the couch, on the page, or both — we can set ourselves free. Therapists are enriched, the page seldom justifies itself — guilt, blame, and analysis provide arid ground for literature — and life itself goes on much as it did before. Except that we grow older and come in for a deal of guilt or blame ourselves. Which can lead us to subscribe, like so many others, to the myth of self-improvement. Only to land us more confused than ever. Striving for maturity can be like striving to be middle class — punishable by success.

The danger for art in all this lies in what one might call the Forrest Gump school of literary endeavour—a cheery little rainbow lens that deems the good "safe" and the bad "dysfunctional," all in a world in which we are surrounded by "choices" if only we could open our eyes and see them. If we could—if those who came before us could themselves have understood things differently—we might now be reading *The Ten Stupid Things Emma Did to Mess Up Her Life,* by Gustave Flaubert; *Women in Love and Their Bad, Bad Choices,* by D. H. Lawrence; *How Happy Families Are Destroyed by Unhappy People,* by Leo Tolstoy.

In the face of all this, I would plead loudly for sticking to the trouble of life—or, rather, to the truth of the trouble of life. What other duty can a writer have? In a culture rendered terrifyingly glib by the rhetoric of lying, one must grasp on to the truth with both hands—embracing what cannot be solved, asking questions to which there can be no answers.

———

"THE UNCONSCIOUS OF most writers remains a dark nursery of anxiety and chaos," said Auden.

Out of the obsessions nursed by such anxiety and chaos comes the life on the page. But how? Certainly not through analysing, however closely. Rather, I would say, it comes through a sort of slow, blind groping after something simmering along the nerves—something that, for want of a better word, one might call "voice." Voice, in this sense, is the writer's equivalent of colour and brushstroke, of chord and discord. Sometimes it is delivered whole; most times it must be struggled for.

Here is V. S. Naipaul on the subject:

It seemed easy and obvious when it had been found, but it had taken me four years to see it. Almost at the same time came the language, the tone, the voice for [the] material. It was as if voice and matter and form were part of one another. . . . To get started as a writer, I had had to go back to the beginning, and pick my way back . . .

to those early literary experiences, some of them not shared by anybody else, which had given me my own view of what lay about me.

It took me any number of mediocre stories and two teething novels before I could pick my own way back. And then, when I did come to the voice and the matter and the form for the story I wanted to write—when I came to where I myself had begun—well, my mother, of course, had come along with me. And so had her voice.

THE WOMEN WHO interest me most, at least for fiction, are those with hot hearts and fierce ambitions—hearts that may include children and ambitions that generally don't. Sometimes such women are artists—self-dramatising women caught between the opposing worlds of artistic daring and material security—sometimes they are not. Whatever the case, theirs is not a problem open to solution. If it were—if a way could be found for a person caught between one self and another, between one need and another, to have both at the same time, with everyone emerging happy and satisfied—well, we would be without sadness in life, without longing, without conflict, and without literature.

As it turned out, my mother's deep, rich baritone was a natural way to introduce a character based on the woman I knew—a woman barely five feet tall and just over a hundred pounds, eternally troubled, wildly ambitious, and essentially bourgeois—a long-nosed sparrow who took herself more seriously than God.

And yet I hadn't even had to give it a thought.

Trying to think a character onto the page is like trying to be funny—bound to fail. In fact, nothing seems to make a writer stupider than thinking. Rational intelligence has little bearing on fictional intelligence; it can make one forget the contradictions inherent in life, the constancy only of surprise. Knowing too much, we find ourselves paralysed by choice—this characteristic or that, this scene or that? In one's ambition or one's vanity, one invokes too much or chooses only those characteristics that are consistent with each other, producing a character that can hardly breathe under the weight of predictability, or one so pieced together that there is no chance of drawing breath at all.

Creating a story that lives on the page, characters that live within it, takes time, endless practise, a measure of luck, and also a sort of pathological refusal to be put off by failure. "Try again. Fail again. Fail better," said Beckett famously—a trajectory that is greatly helped, I think, by the assurance of a skilled, well-intentioned, and unfailingly honest audience.

In my case, that audience was, first and last, my mother. And still there she is, looking up from the page to say, "But why should I care about this person, whoever she is?" It took me a long time to understand that if there wasn't an answer to that question, I didn't have a character at all. And that that was my objection to almost all of her productions—they could not make me care.

I had had a long apprenticeship in performance myself, not only onstage—which I
loathed much more than I did being stuck in the
audience—but also at home. "Can you do
Irish?" I'd hear my mother bark at someone who
had come for an audition. "North Country?
Welsh? Russian? Well, what can you do?" Pause.
"All right"—*sigh*—"Let's hear your American.
Read this."

We ourselves were a family of mimics, often
cruel with each other, always honest. "Dreadful!" someone would shout. "Miles off!" my
mother would add, getting up to go. Fail, and
you died on the spot. Anyone was fair game for
an attempt, even she. Especially she.

Having spent a childhood draped across her
study chair, reading Oscar Wilde—which I was
allowed to do as long as I didn't guffaw and interrupt the timing of her scripts—I first settled
her into a version of Lady Bracknell. Never
witty herself, my mother could easily appreciate
wit in others—certainly in Wilde. My sisters
took her on in other ways, but it was Lady

Bracknell that she preferred. Of course she did; she felt herself increased by Wilde, as indeed she was. What she did not love were jokes, and so, in a family of practical jokers and raconteurs, she was always the odd man out, always the straight man finding the rest of us "just a little bit silly, if you ask me."

And yet this was the woman who would drop me off at a friend's house on a Saturday afternoon, carrying the enormous reel-to-reel tape recorder on which she and my father recorded their productions of *Lux Radio Theatre*. The friend and I would install the contraption in her music room, where the telephone sat. And then I would dial up Mr. Kaplan, our Hebrew teacher, taking on the part of Mrs. Horsley-Uppington, Chairlady of the Protestant Ladies' Society for the Prevention of Discontent Among the Upper Orders. It was always I who did the talking; my friend, now a corporate lawyer on Long Island, held the microphone and worked the recorder. In a loud horsey voice, I would command Mr. Kaplan to attend our next monthly tea. What we required, I told him, was a brief—"very brief, if you please, Mr. Kaplan, shall we say five minutes?—a five-minute précis of your Jewish dietary laws. 'Kasho'? Is that what it's called? But Mr. Kaplan, none of your palavering on all afternoon, please—we have no time for that sort of thing, you know."

All Mr. Kaplan's protests, all his attempts to explain that such a thing was not possible, lady, were shouted down in the bluff, barking tones of a British colonial matron.

And then, the bit between the teeth, on we would go to the next victim, and then the next.

When I got home, we would gather in the lounge—my mother, my father, and I. After the drinks tray had been brought in, they would sit back with a Scotch while I ran the tape back—both of them roaring with delight as Mrs. Horsley-Uppington bullied Mr. Kaplan, survivor of Auschwitz, yet again.

Had I been thinking up a character like my mother roaring back on that couch like that—had I been thinking up any character at all, however based—I might never have come to the odd and contradictory combination of characteristics that I have been trying to illustrate here. When I did come finally to write her, I simply knew without thinking that I had a character who, even though she may not have found jokes funny, had as keen an appreciation of cruelty as any comic. And who also, oddly enough, had perfect comic timing herself.

At home, under the beam of her increasing regard, I began to extend Lady Bracknell into other modes and forms of satire. Once, I sang her, quite improbably, into a version of Sophie Tucker's "My Yiddishe Mama." But she only advised me to give it up. I had the accent all wrong, she said, and anyway what did I know of Yiddishe mothers? Like Sophie Tucker, she herself had had a much belovèd Yiddishe mother, a saint, she said, without a word of English. It was her father who wasn't a good man, not at all. He was a drinker and a womaniser, and he stole the housekeeping money from her mother's underwear drawer to give to the new housekeeper, on whom he had designs.

The idea of this—the money in the underwear, the housekeeper coming in—this stayed with me for years, as did the bitter tone of her voice as she told me that story. (Later, in her own old age, she herself began imagining my father stealing money from her underwear drawer, her maid sprinkling poisoned powder on the sheets of her bed.) Her bitterness was still with me when I wrote a story—later to become a novel—in the voice of that housekeeper, seizing ruthlessly on the memory itself, riding it wildly, falling so easily into the voice and person of that young housekeeper that she might have been myself describing my mother as Sarah Frank—twelve years old this time and full of bitter resentment towards her father's paramour.

I am not sure what my mother would have made of this story. She was fiercely loyal in life, trusting no one outside the family, and not many within it either. Still, once life was transformed into art, the only sin to be considered was failure. In the daily theatrical round of our lives, when I myself would come up as the object of caricature by one of my sisters, she wouldn't scold the sister; rather, she would show me how I could walk into a room so as not to invite such ridicule. Right up until her decline, she tried to coach me out of what she considered my "ghastly little voice." "What they must think of you in America, I can't imagine," she would say. "You chirrup and gabble in that dreadful accent. They probably don't understand a word you're saying."

"I WONDER," WROTE George Eliot in *Daniel Deronda,* "whether one oftener learns to love real objects through their representations, or the representations through the real objects." I wonder too. I cannot now easily remember the mother I had before I began sizing her up for reinvention. As soon as I did—as soon as I began to shift her into caricature, and then, much later, onto the page — the woman herself became both subject and audience, mother and child. Even in my notes, written seconds after observation, she would become someone seen by strangers. And still she is my creature.

Is it possible, I wonder, to stare into the chasm of life without being blinded? Or does one need a filter, just as one needs a photographic negative to observe an eclipse of the sun? Perhaps, after all, such a filter is one of the great gifts of literature itself — both of reading it and of writing it.

Considering her childhood, Marguerite Duras writes:

In books I've written about my childhood, I can't remember, suddenly, what I left out, what I said. I think I wrote about our love for our mother, but I don't know if I wrote about how we hated her too, or about our love for one another, and our terrible hatred too, in that common family history of ruin and death which was ours whatever happened, in love or in hate, and which I still can't understand however hard I try, which is still beyond my reach, hidden in the very depths of my flesh, blind as a new-born child. It's the area on whose brink silence begins.

It is against the brink of such silence, such darkness, that one pushes fiction, using words, images, metaphors, to create a shape for a character, for life itself. The process is one that approaches control, but it is a control achieved out of chaos. And the result is a sort of knowledge — a knowledge that comes with the writing, not before it.

In my case, the apprenticeship for the character of my mother in all its various manifestations took over thirty years and is still ongoing. Even now, committing her once again into words, I find myself leaving out the bits that don't fit for this purpose — the less wild, less endearing, less dramatic, less funny bits — but the ones that are nevertheless just as true.

And yet, why her? Why not my father, a man who could have given Nancy Mitford's General Murgatroyd a trot for his money? Because of my father, our household was run by any number of bizarre rules and requirements. One of these was having each of his daughters turn to him at the end of dinner to say, "Thank you God for my lovely supper; please may I leave the table?" To which he would nod his regal head. On a Sunday, after tea, we were to gather on the lower lawn for cricket—the insect, not the game. The singing of crickets disturbed his sleep, he said. And so we were each handed an oil can and a hammer, and, for the next hour or so, were to search out the cricket holes, pour oil down them, and then, when the crickets crawled out, bash them to death with the hammer.

Why did I push all this upstage? I don't really know, unless, perhaps, it was because my mother just grabbed the footlights for herself. She was wilder, more passionate, less easily pleased, more honest, less consistent, and more difficult to live with. As she played her own life, so I played her on the page. Perhaps this was it. Or perhaps it was the love affair she conducted with trouble — perhaps she was just more trouble in the way trouble counted for me. Which brings me back to all those writers who killed off the mothers of their girls. The romance of their stories was the romance of the man. Mothers would certainly have told the story a different way.

I wonder now how different my own story would have been had my mother not loved me as she did — child of her middle age, the one who most resembled her (nose, temper, ambition). Narcissism abounding? Of course. But then such a diagnosis is not much help for fiction, and not much for life either. "Be careful how you interpret life," said Howard Nemerov. "It's like that."

I did not interpret; and still I don't. And yet I cannot help worrying this particular question, wondering whether the answer lurks, as does so much in fiction, around trouble — the sort of trouble that my mother both caused and suffered in the small bowl in which she had chosen

to confine herself. It was a trouble full of passion, cruelty, delusion, and moments of truth—
a trouble driven, at least in part, by her refusal to
be pleased by anything short of triumph.

At some point, as I was edging myself out
of childhood and into her peripheral vision—
prizes won, things written, people noticing—
her fierce ambitions began to attach themselves
to me. At the same time she was the canny wife
and mother, who understood quite well how to
negotiate for herself and her daughters in a
world run by men—a bourgeois who could be
deeply unsettled by the word "divorcée."

All this I put into another of her appear-
ances, laughing as I wrote. I had long since
achieved a version of the life I had longed for—
leaving and returning had become the rhythm
and substance of that life. And always my mother
was in the front row of the audience, my father
beside her. We were like lovers, the three of
us, and yet it was she from whom I had had to
wrench myself most fiercely; she who kept encouraging me to go. Long before I understood

it as such, I had absorbed the role of audience in our lives. It was the great lie by which we lived, and also the only truth. And yet it took the writing of *Home Ground* for me to understand just how deeply it ran.

When I had finished the first draft of that novel, I received a letter from an editor in New York. "I believe you are writing a memoir," she wrote. "If you don't have a publisher, I would very much like to see it."

I phoned my agent immediately. "Do not send out a first draft," she barked. "Never send out a first draft."

This was not the answer I wanted. So I phoned a few friends. "Send it right now," they said, "but make sure she knows it's a novel, not a memoir."

And so I did. And, after a month or so, back it came with a three-page letter. The material, said the editor, was fascinating, what a bizarre world I had written about. But it was not yet a novel—nothing tied the scenes together except chronology. What it needed, she said, was a focus. If I could rewrite it with this in mind, she'd be glad to take another look.

For the next few months, I became obsessed with focus, word and concept. What was it? How would I find it? I drove myself so mad with questions that the word itself lost all meaning. *Focus, focus, focus*—two syllables that meant nothing. So I wrote out all the scenes in the novel on three-by-five cards, dozens of them, and spread them around on the dining-room floor, searching for a pattern. I could find none — nothing but the chronology of a girl growing up in an eccentric theatrical family in South Africa in the fifties and sixties.

Finally, and in desperation, I took my problem to a friend. She had been a diction and acting coach at the Met, and was now out to pasture with the San Francisco Opera. She read the manuscript, and then looked up at me as if I were mad. "But it's obvious," she said. "The focus for the story is the theatre."

The theatre. It was such a commonplace in our lives that I had not even noticed it. But, once I did, I saw that she was right. There it was through and through. It was not the subject of the story—rather it was the axis around which the story turned. And audience itself was endemic to it.

My mother herself found nothing to object to in the novel except the fact that I had given her a booming voice. "I do not boom!" she boomed. I was immensely relieved. When she had read my first novel, she had pronounced it far too full of "carrying-on." "Ugly, darling," she said, "all that carrying-on." I'd told myself then that she was a prude, which indeed she was. But, when the time came for *Home Ground,* I rather dreaded what I'd be in for.

As it turned out, she didn't seem to notice any carrying-on, or, if she did, didn't seem to mind. I came to understand that the "carrying-on" of the first novel had been written in the spirit either of romance or revenge, both of which can make one feel one shouldn't be watching. By contrast, in the bizarre world of *Home Ground*—a world utterly familiar to her,

even in its blur of imagined and remembered experience — the carrying-on must have vanished
into the story.

A FEW YEARS ago, I was asked to write a memoir: my mother, my daughter, myself. I have no
objections to memoir, and, in fact, I did make a
valiant effort; I wanted the money. But, as I
wrote, I kept finding it difficult to breathe. This
was not, I think, due to a fear of exposure: fiction exposes one to scrutiny every bit as fierce
as does memoir. It was, rather, that I felt I'd
been sent to jail. Even though I had the living
and breathing models for my subjects at my
command, I found myself trying to think them
up on the page. Worse than this, I was trying to
squash into them everything I knew. And, worse
still, I couldn't bring myself to believe that it
mattered.

But worst of all was trying to render my
daughter. This was not because I worried about
what she'd find out—we had between us a

version of the same complex and ruthless habit of truth and lies as I'd had with my own mother—but because, despite the fact that she had been born when I was twenty-four, she was too new in my life, too solid and yet also unknowable and unknown.

From the start, performance was the liveliest thing between us. It enlivened what would otherwise have been a dreary game: policeman and delinquent. In another life, being wed to order and control, I'd probably have been able to relax into the role of policeman. But then I felt panicked by the part, enraged by the small demands and relentless provocations of a child—blocked, challenged, circumscribed, nailed down.

Apart from all else, this was motherhood such as my own mother had never experienced. And nor, by extension, had I. There were no nannies, no cooks, no housecleaners, none of that. Neither were there grandparents and aunts and uncles and cousins. And, beyond them, no society to whom we were known. Like so many others in this country, we were alone, the two of us, day after day—prisoner and guard. It was a silence such as I had never known.

And then, one day, she laughed—probably in terror; she was an infant and I was swinging her up and down on my leg—and I grabbed her up and loved her fiercely.

Perhaps that's when it began—the idea of a person in the audience—hers for me, mine for her. Audience again.

Once, when she was two, and conducting a tantrum on a street corner in San Francisco, I broke into a flamenco dance around her, stamping, yowling, clapping, singing. She shut up and laughed. Once, I tore her passport in half. Once, I drove the car pool in a devil mask and bridal veil. Once, I threw her clothes out of the window. Once, I locked her out of a hotel room and she had to bring in the Mexican police to break down the door.

These were the theatrics, the tales to be told later. But what of the furies? The savagery? The threats? The flailing of the wooden spoon, thwack? Shoulders and arms grabbed, hers and mine? Our voices rising into bellows of insults? Truths uttered in rage? Most of all that rage and those truths? Echoes of another life.

"When you are old," she once shouted up at me, "I won't push your wheelchair."

And yet now she dreams of keeping me in a little cottage at the bottom of her garden and dressing me in animal prints. She is like a lover herself, or a doting nanny—watchful, exacting, jealous of her claim. I too am watchful, careful to keep myself free. She lives across the globe and reports in daily for my audience. I see the surprise, the strange interest she takes in the decline of my body. She is new to beauty, thrilled with it.

And still, I am my mother, loving the sight of a lovely thing—arms, legs, hands, face. I am my mother, watching my mother in her—the worship of style, the love of a good scene, the value of outrage, the keen sense of the authentic.

"I always knew that you loved me," she says.

"Don't confuse anxiety with love," I reply, knowing that she will laugh.

———

QUITE SOON, I gave up trying for memoir and returned to fiction. My daughter was nowhere to be seen; she never has been. But I did plunder what I had written of my mother and I used it for a wild new character I was creating—a diva, marooned at the bottom of Africa, a mad-woman, survivor of Auschwitz, demon mother, possessive maniac, and keeper of secrets unto the grave.

MUSGRAVE HOUSE

IT MUST BE LIKE THIS FOR THE PARENT who left after the divorce — standing at the front door, ringing the bell to be let in. Worse, perhaps. The people who live here now are not even enemies; they are strangers. More than this, they are proud strangers. They have welcomed us back, my oldest sister and me, to see the restoration they have performed on our old house. They have even given it a name it never had. It is etched in glass over the front door: MUSGRAVE HOUSE. All the vulgarities of the interim owners have been thrown out, the new owner assures us as she ushers us in—the marble flooring, the wet bar, the modern this, and up-to-date that. The house is back to what it was, she says. Restored.

But how could she know, this new owner, that the house we grew up in, that our father grew up in before us, could make no sense to restoration-minded people? My grandmother's old boudoir, for instance, the cavernous corner room in which my parents kept their theatre costumes—two vast chests and three wardrobes stuffed with ostrich-feather capes, buckled boots, buttoned boots, bustles, parasols, togas, spats, old telephones, hats upon hats, and beards, wigs, costume jewelry—is it a boudoir again, with its view of the sea, its battered chaise longue, balding pink carpet, and flowered wallpaper?

And what about the pantries? The cake pantry, the flower pantry, the silver pantry, and the crockery pantry? Cupboards upon cupboards filled with services for seventy-two in milk; seventy-two more in meat; shelves deep enough for huge silver salvers, meat covers, platters, glasses by the dozens and dozens? What about the linen closet with its layers and layers of tablecloths in different lengths? And the tables themselves? The candles lit in the candelabras? The party about to begin?

The house was perfect for parties. With its vast hall, huge dining room, sitting room, breakfast room, study, and the deep verandah that faced out over the city and the bay, it could accommodate hundreds and very often did. There were theatre parties and engagement parties, soirées, Friday nights, Jewish holidays. Every week or so, twenty or more members of the family settled themselves around the dining-room table, with the children parceled off to the breakfast room if necessary. Servants were borrowed, sized up, poached. There were fights, grudges, infidelities, doorbells ringing at odd hours, and muffled conversations.

My mother ran the parties as she staged her plays—instructing, adjusting for effect, arranging the timing, editing the menu she was handed on a slate by the cook. The parties themselves exercised a power over her that none of us possessed: they could draw her out of one of her intolerable sulks. There she would stand next to my father, to whom she might not have spoken for a week, slipping her arm through his as the doorbell rang, leading him forward with a smile, her cigarette waving. "*Daahhhling!* Hello! Hel*lo*!"

The domestic theatre of our lives seemed to rely on a constant flow of visitors—players or audience, either would do. Actors and actresses, friends, family—they would come to stay for weeks or even months. When cousins came down from Johannesburg for the July holidays, beds would be moved into the boudoir for the boys, others placed out on the sleeping porch for the overflow. The three of us would be moved about ourselves: me onto the divan in my father's dressing room, my sisters, under protest, in together with a cousin or two.

With boys in the house, everything changed among us. Their noise and swagger usurped my own role as honorary son, and I found myself casting about madly for a way to cope with the ruinous teasing, the horseplay, the smells and leers, the charge in the air as they sauntered to the bathroom half naked — the delicious promise of what lay ahead in life.

Usually the only males in the house other than my father were servants, and they hardly seemed to count. Crossing the border into their quarters was my first venture into foreign territory. Again and again, and against my mother's orders, I slipped in there, squatting with the men to watch them smoke their homemade cigarettes, sitting on my nanny's bed as she ate her lunch. I knew it was rude, that they couldn't tell me to get out, but I went in anyway, bringing with me little things from the house that wouldn't be missed — an old hairbrush, a florist's bow, a few cigarettes, a bottle of beer. And then the housekeeper would call from the kitchen window. "Hey! You! Nuisance! Come! Your mother wants to fit you!"

Every year, my mother sewed each of us two new dresses, drafting the patterns, choosing the materials, leaving large hems so that they could be handed down. The house itself had once received this sort of attention from her, too. Some of the furniture and most of the curtains my parents had taken over from my grandparents — stripping, varnishing, recovering, rearranging. The rest they bought at auctions in the first full flush of ownership. Once it was all in place, however, they turned their attention to edibles and wearables. If the roof needed tiling, if springs went awry in one of our mattresses, they found a way of making do — patching over the bald spot, turning over the mattress.

Most of the crockery was simple stuff in stock patterns, chipped and crazed by servants over the years. The glass wasn't crystal; the silver largely plate, much of it dulling through from use. The rooms were always in need of some paint, the brocades and linens fading and worn, the down pulverising, the curtains perishing in the hot subtropical sun. Deep gouges had been scratched into the doors by dogs wanting to come in or go out. The dogs, in fact, were everywhere — on the furniture and under it, in our beds, roaring down to the front door as the guests arrived laughing and shouting, in voices trained to carry.

"Daaahling!" "Nigel! You were *simply* marvellous!"

The theatre parties started well after midnight on the last night of the run, and went on, sometimes, till dawn. Up the back stairs, to the old nursery, where I slept, came the noises and smells from the kitchen — the cook shouting orders, baby chickens out of the oven, gravied rice and mushrooms, honey-glazed carrots, and homemade breads carried down the long dark corridor, past the pantries, from the kitchen to the dining room. And then Cedric, a producer who had no children of his own, would come upstairs to fetch me, to carry me down into the lights and the crowd.

THE NEW OWNER smiles at my oldest sister. At the age of nineteen, this sister married and moved around the corner into an even bigger house, on more ground. When my father ran out of money and had to put our house up for sale, he offered it to her, but she didn't want it. To me, it was obvious that she didn't want to come back, to be the one to carry on. She is the least theatrical person I know. I watch how she takes care not to look around too curiously. Perhaps she just isn't curious. She has spent her life wishing she were as far away as possible, while I, who live halfway around the world, cannot seem to stop coming back. Our middle sister, big on dramatic flair, wouldn't even come to look at the house. "I've seen it once," she says. "That was quite enough."

The woman is carrying on about the wrought iron balustrade they have restored on the staircase, the brass stair rods that they had to order from overseas. They are having the original blueprints framed, she says, her husband found them in a dusty archive in the basement of the city hall. I should be glad, I know. I have seen the house twice before, during previous incarnations. But with its marble flooring, huge porcelain dogs, gilded cornucopias, fountains, wet bars, and other grotesqueries, it seemed then only to be hiding.

In a way, I pity her, this new owner, with her balustrades and stair rods and blueprints. She has our silence to contend with, the judgment it seems to bring down on her head. My sister is quiet by nature, comfortable with silence. I am not. Usually, I jabber on in order to put people at their ease. I tell stories, look for common ground.

Now, however, I am deprived of speech. I see the floors, sanded smooth and finished to a gloss; the banister, stripped and oiled; brass switch plates polished; the glass-paneled doors to the breakfast room painted white. But, with all its neat arrangements and standard coordinations, its photoready angles and gleaming surfaces, the house is not even vulgar anymore. It has become commonplace.

Botanical prints, identically framed and matted in a soft moss green to match the runner, rise with the stairs. A neat flower arrangement, still girded by its florist's bow, sits on a small table where our vast Cape Dutch chest had stood. We, too, had had flowers in that spot, every week a billowing profusion of whatever came out of the garden—huge fronds and ferns and coloured leaves, or an arrangement of green hydrangeas, agapanthus, anthuriums, dahlias, cannas, and always the odd caterpillar or locust or praying mantis waiting to jump out—the whole mélange reflected in the enormous mirror that hung behind the chest.

Without that chest, that mirror, and the other smaller Chinese chest next to the front door, where the telephone lived, without the dogs roiling around on the Persian rugs and someone on the phone covering the mouthpiece and shouting, "SHUT UP!," the hall does indeed make sense. I see the distances as they must have been intended by the architect—the clear path from the front door to the sitting room, from the bottom of the stairs to the cloakroom door.

"We took out those awful hanging lights," says the new owner, pointing up to a light fitting lost in the space it inhabits. "We had that chandelier specially made."

I look up. There, two stories above, the moulded ceiling still seems to float like the sky, up to the milky skylight. Once again, the stairs circle out of sight, the upstairs balconies, front and back, seem to be waiting for an opera of shouts and yells, upstairs to downstairs or across the space between them.

Suddenly, I remember that the palm trees are gone from the front, all six or seven that used to run the length of the wrought iron fence, their trunks entwined with elephant ears. Who cut them down? And who took out the fence itself? Who built the high white wall that hides the house from the street? And who put in the fishpond that I seem to have noticed without even noticing on my way in?

"Shall we have tea on the verandah before we look around?" the new owner asks, smiling uneasily at me. She must have heard about the fuss my second novel caused—the family exposed, our lives, this house itself all over the place. She leads us through the sitting room—perfectly coordinated now in peach and cream, with two seating areas, wall-to-wall carpeting, balloon curtains, more florist's flowers—to a wicker couch ensemble outside, the tea tray laid out on a table in the middle.

By now, I can see that my sister is alarmed by my quietness. She has begun to engage the new owner in chat—the last meeting of the gourmet club, the private school situation. Down below us, where the cricket lawn used to be, is a swimming pool and a pool house. As a child, I had nagged for a pool down there, any pool. I would even dig it myself, I had said. But they had just laughed. "What's wrong with the sea?" my father would ask. "Who wants to swim in a pool when you can swim in the sea?"

Me. I did. I wanted somewhere in which we could all swim together, just us, no strangers. I wanted my parents home for dinner, like other parents, not off to rehearsals every evening. I wanted us to spend our holidays in a caravan, not at the mountain resort where children had to eat in a separate dining room. The whole idea of a caravan holiday seemed wonderfully cosy to me, fictional almost: the family all in one place, sharing things, even dinner, and everyone with little tasks to do, no one out of earshot.

But I knew it was hopeless. We weren't that sort of family. And my mother was handicapped for caravan living. She couldn't cook. Nor, I presume, could she wash clothes, or iron, or clean. Only in her bedroom had I ever seen her out of stockings and heels. And, anyway, we were always fighting—my mother with my father, them with us, us with each other. It was a house of isolated dramas and conflagrations—kitchen, study, bedrooms—voices raised, doors slammed, shouts, whisperings, thick-walled silences. Had it not been built of stone and brick, with large grounds around it, the ructions and the insults would have carried across town. As it was, my friend, the girl next door, once asked me—after a particularly loud fight for dominance of the bathroom—whether I'd ever been strapped for swearing. Strapped? Such a thing was unheard of in our house. Physical violence was not our way. We practised insult and slander instead.

Only when we were apart did peace reign— my mother in her study, timing scripts; my father listening to himself on the radio in the sitting room; upstairs, my middle sister hogging the boudoir phone while the oldest was hiding in the sewing room, watching for her fiancé. And me flying around the garden with the dogs or crawling under the house, exploring the dark, tortuous rooms there that were inhabited by rats. Or climbing to the top of the mango tree to survey the world as I knew it.

———

TEA IS OVER and the new owner suggests a tour. We follow her to an enormous gourmet kitchen, which seems to have swallowed up the pantries. From it, we can see the tennis court they have blasted into the hill behind the house, deep and frightening like a quarry. The old servants' quarters have been blasted out, too, and the laundry room, and the mulberry tree I almost stripped when I set my silkworms free on it. In fact, I realise suddenly, all the trees are gone — palms, flamboyants, mangoes, naartjies, pawpaws, avocado pears. There's hardly any real garden left. No monkeys snatching the fruit either, I presume; no dogs jumping after them.

We walk up to the gaming room in the old garage — billiards and card tables and the smell of cigars. And then, coming around the front again, we descend slate stairs to the wine cellar, built under the house. It is well stocked and temperature-controlled, the owner says. Beyond it is a gym, with exercycles and weights and pulleys, a doctor's scale, fluorescent light. It is impossible now to imagine the wild and mysterious place that this once was—the lawnmowers and sacks of seed, old dolls' prams, rakes, scythes, and, farther in, the dark rooms and corridors of red earth.

Back in the house, following our hostess upstairs, I run my hand along the banister to feel the contours, the upward twists at the corners. The scratches have been sanded out. So have the long grooves carved by generations of zips and buttons sliding down, bump, to the bottom, late for supper.

Through the dark passage to the back bedrooms we go. It has been lighted now and is almost charming with its vaulted ceiling and mouldings I have never seen before. As a child, I ran the gauntlet of that dark passage every night, waiting for my middle sister to jump out of the shadows with a screech and a torch lighting a hideous grimace from below. We were a family of violent jokers—exposed bottoms sliced with a hand, buckets of water poured from an upstairs window, elaborate ruses, wild denouements.

"Do you have children?" I ask. Are they allowed to play violent games? I want to know. Jump out of windows? Slide down the banisters?

Suddenly, the woman laughs. Her husband, she says, used to walk past the house on his way home from school, vowing again and again that one day he would own it.

I try to smile with her at his triumph, but I can only think of how completely and for all these years I have owned this house myself. It is the axis around which the compass of my life has turned: there in the clang of a wrought iron gate, the whiff of frangipani, palm trees in a hot wind, coarse grass on a Mexican beach. It has come with me everywhere I have been. It is in everything I write.

She opens the door to the old nursery, my old room. My mad aunt had been in here before me, her singing wafting out through the fanlight. "The fanlights are gone," I say. "Oh, fanlights!" cries the new owner happily, "No one has fanlights anymore, now that there is air-conditioning."

I hadn't thought of that. I stare into the room as it is now. Indeed there are children. This is the girl's room, done out in pink and yellow, with stuffed animals and frilly pillows, pillows, pillows. My sisters' rooms have been combined into the boy's room, wood-paneled and blue. Each has its own bathroom. No fighting, I presume. Or cursing. Or swearing.

Standing at the door to my parents' old bedroom, I steal a look at my sister, but she is fixed into her public smile. It is the smile she used to wear when we came in to be inspected before we left for school—my mother in her bed jacket, reading scripts; my father at the breakfast tray, his silk scarf tied around his head like a pirate's. We watch the owner demonstrate the vast master bed. For some reason, it has been raised onto a platform, like a throne. Beside the padded bedstead is a panel of buttons. They control the whole house, she tells us—lights, TV, music, intercoms, bells to the kitchen, burglar alarm.

The owner's smile itself is losing a little of its starch. Clearly, she has conducted this tour many times before, but not for such an audience. We have heard that they have stretched their finances to the limit restoring this place, that, if things don't improve in the economy, they might well have to put it up for sale. It is a threat we heard often ourselves as children — the upkeep, the staff, the running, the ridiculous prices of everything.

Our hostess leads on, through my father's dressing room, now her husband's study, to the old boudoir. There she throws the door open and stands back. "We started here," she says, going in to open the door of the armoire, revealing a TV hidden within. "The bathroom is en suite," she points out. And, indeed it is — clean towels, pristine soaps. There is also a curtained bedside table, a chair in the same material, curtains too. I have seen this material in good hotels. It is male or female, young or old.

I slide out onto the upstairs verandah, and they follow. Isn't the view wonderful? they ask each other. Until this moment, however, I have never thought of this as a "view" — ships waiting to come into the harbour, yachts tacking into the wind, the bluff blue-grey and the city white in the afternoon sun. I have stood here as a girl of thirteen or fourteen, staring out and wondering about my life. How I would spring myself from this place at the bottom of the world, from these people I loved and hated? And where could I go? And when, when, when?

I move off to the far end of the verandah to look down over the front lawn—I can see the fishpond now—and suddenly I understand that the house itself has nothing to do with fishponds and balustrades, that it can slip easily from under the weight of a schoolboy's ambition. Any number of schoolboys could come along to restore it, or to lock it up and leave it behind, knock it down completely, build over it. And still the top of the flamboyant would be close enough for me to make the leap onto this parapet. The dogs would run in a pack along the fence, up and down. The screaming and slamming would have me lying on the bench in the summerhouse, waiting it out until the fuss was over.

NOT MUCH OF A FUNERAL

WHEN YOU GOT TO THAT PAGE IN THE galleys, Dad, and you looked up and said, "Didn't give me much of a funeral, did you?" I laughed. We have always understood the joke that fiction plays on life—you, me, Ma, the three of us. But, oh, the joke is on me now, isn't it?

Standing dry-eyed at your funeral, and Ma quite mad in the wheelchair beside me — mad or playing mad; once she started slipping, none of us knew the difference, not even you — standing there in the heat and damp of summer, with the men chanting in Hebrew, and a lawnmower somewhere, an African whistling, Kikuyu grass and flamboyants and Indian mynahs, I could only think how ordinary it all was — eleven o'clock in the morning, people glancing at their watches.

Putting that funeral onto the page was more difficult, weeping as I wrote, as if I were getting it right.

But I didn't get it right. Writing someone else standing at that funeral was quite different. She had known this death was coming; she had always known. I might have known too, but I refused. Year after year, Ma kept saying, "Don't leave it too long before you come back." And I didn't. Every year I came home, like the fondest of lovers. We were lovers, the three of us. When you told me her mind was slipping, I changed the subject. I wanted nothing about us to slip away.

But then, standing at the graveside among the mourners, I thought I must be slipping myself when Nicholas grabbed the spade, thinking it was his job as usual to do the work, and the rabbi had to stop him. Who could have thought that up? I glanced at the others for a smile, but they were crying hopelessly. They knew there's no refusing any of this.

When I had phoned you in the hospital from the other side of the world and asked, "Shall I come out now?," you said, "I'll let you know when." And then, one day, I just said, "I'm coming, on Tuesday," and you said, "Thank you." I might have known then what was coming. All the way out, plane after plane, it was as if I were flying back from the funeral already, taking with me everything I could think of, like a refugee. Our drives through the sugarcane on a Sunday afternoon, me steering. The smell of your sweat after golf. And of gum arabic as you sat at the mirror, pasting on a beard, strand by strand. And of Pond's cold cream, and of Lake number nine—all those powders and paints lined up in the makeup tray. And your Brylcreem, and your Knight's Castile, and light starch only in your shirts. Your clothes laid out on the divan in your dressing room—wool, linen, cotton, everything 100 percent. And your dressing gowns, and your smoking jackets, your hairbrushes, your clothes brushes, and your silk cravats. Your elegance spoiled me for elegant men, Dad, your beauty for beauty, your manners, your utter English decency.

And if you were fiercely jealous of the men who came to take us away, each one of us, only we knew of this. If we told people that you bellowed and slammed doors and called us "blithering, unimaginative blockheads," they thought it funny. It was funny, until you had to cope with Ma, and the bellowing didn't help, and she didn't know what you were talking about anyway, or pretended she didn't, and called you a Jekyll and Hyde, which, in a sense, you were.

I put all that into the novels too, but still you came out less vivid than she. I seemed to give her all the best lines. Or she just took them. That's the way she was.

There are things I forgot, though, like the way you'd lose your voice just before opening night. And how Ma would go mad with the understudy, and you'd be swallowing raw eggs, and have us whispering around the dinner table. And then every time, every time, back it would come — the low growl, the fake purr you used on ticket ladies and usherettes, and they always gave you the best seats in the house.

And once I came into your bathroom and found Nicholas brushing his beard with your special nailbrush, and of course I couldn't tell you because no one but you was ever allowed to use that special nailbrush — or that special pair of scissors, or those special tweezers, or that special anything — and, for all I knew, he used your special linen face towel to clean the toilet. You would have laughed if you had read that in the galleys. You would have looked up and said, "Only you could have thought this up!"

After the funeral, one of my old lovers phoned me, the one I'd loved longer than any other. He phoned to say that he'd only just heard, and how sorry he was. But I didn't recognise his voice anymore; he had to repeat his name three times. You would have liked that too, Dad. You loathed the sight and the sound of him, even though he was the one who told me again and again, over all the years, that I should hold on tight to both of you; you'd be leaving sooner than I thought. I listened when he said this. He belonged to the Chevra Kadisha; he understood how quickly a person can lock up and go away, leaving nothing behind to come home to.

I listened, and, really, I did understand. I had always understood. What I couldn't bear was the thought of this, now: talking into nothing, nothing coming back. This horrible joke. This dead air.

ACKNOWLEDGMENTS

"A Child's Reading" was first published in the *Washington Post Book World* and then reprinted in *Bookworms: Great Writers and Readers Celebrate Reading,* Laura Furman and Elinore Standard, eds., Carroll & Graf Publishers, in 1997. "Honorary Son" was first published in *Allure,* September 1994. "Sex with the Servants" was first published, in much shorter form, in *The Confidence Woman: 26*

Women Writers at Work, Eve Shelnutt, ed., Long-
street Press, in June 1991, and then in *Tin House
Magazine,* Spring 2002. "False Starts and Creative
Failure" was first published as "False Starts" in
the *Threepenny Review,* December 1999. "Embrac-
ing the Alien" was first published, in much
shorter form, in *Becoming American: Personal Es-
says by First Generation Immigrant Women,* Meri
Nana-Ama Danquah, ed., Hyperion, and then
by *Southwest Review,* Winter 2003. "Home on the
Range" was first published as "Call Home" in
I've Always Meant to Tell You: Letters to Our Mothers,
Constance Warloe, ed., Pocket Books. "The Big
Snore" was first published in the *New York Times
Magazine,* Dec. 4, 1988. "Doing Time" was published in *Harper's Magazine,* August 2005. "Taming the Gorgon" was first published in the
Georgia Review, Winter 2003. "Musgrave House"
was first published, in shorter form, as "Without the Mango Tree," in *House Beautiful* and then
reprinted in *House and Leisure,* South Africa, Oc-
tober 1993 and reprinted later in *Thoughts of
Home: Reflections on Families, Houses, and Homelands*

from the Pages of House Beautiful, Hearst Books, 1995. "Not Much of a Funeral" was first published in *From Daughters & Sons to Fathers: What I've Never Said,* Constance Warloe, ed., Story Line Press.